HOLLAND
BELGIUM & LUXEMBOURG

Welcome to
Holland, Belgium and Luxembourg

Carole Chester

Collins
Glasgow and London

The author and publishers wish to acknowledge
the generous assistance of:
Pierre Claus,
Director of the Belgian National Tourist Office;
Edo Marx,
Director of the Netherlands National Tourist Office;
Jim Christen,
Director of the Luxembourg National Tourist Office.

Cover Photographs

Van Phillips
(top; Alkmaar cheese market, top left: traditional
costume in Volendam, top right: Amsterdam
mid left: lace making, Bruges, mid right: Friesland,
bottom right: Clervaux.)

Photographs

All by Van Phillips except;
pp. 82 (btm), 91 (top), 101, 105
Belgian National Tourist Office

Regional Maps

Mike Shand

Town Plans

M. & R. Piggot

Illustrations

pp 6–7 Peter Joyce

First published 1982
Revised edition 1986
Copyright © Carole Chester
Published by William Collins Sons and Company Limited
Printed in Great Britain

ISBN 0 00 447383 3

HOW TO USE THIS BOOK

The contents page of this book shows how the countries are divided up into tourist regions. The book is in two sections; general information and gazetteer. The latter is arranged in the tourist regions with an introduction and a regional map (detail below left). There are also plans of the main cities (detail below right). All the towns and villages in the gazetteer are shown on the regional maps. Places to visit and leisure facilities available in each region and city are indicated by symbols. Main roads, railways and airports are shown on the maps and plans.

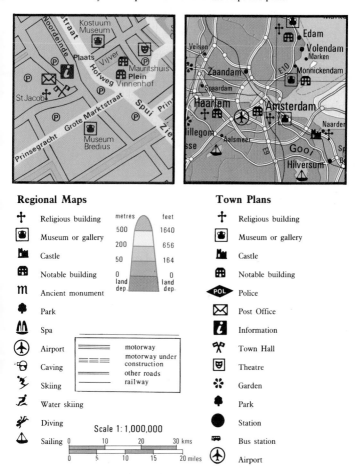

Regional Maps

† Religious building

▣ Museum or gallery

🏰 Castle

⊞ Notable building

m Ancient monument

♠ Park

⋔ Spa

✈ Airport

⊖ Caving

🎿 Skiing

Water skiing

Diving

⛵ Sailing

metres	feet
500	1640
200	656
50	164
0 land dep.	0 land dep.

═══	motorway
══	motorway under construction
—	other roads
—	railway

Scale 1: 1,000,000

0   10   20   30 kms
0   5   10   15   20 miles

Town Plans

† Religious building

▣ Museum or gallery

🏰 Castle

⊞ Notable building

POL Police

✉ Post Office

i Information

✄ Town Hall

☺ Theatre

✽ Garden

♠ Park

● Station

🚌 Bus station

✈ Airport

CONTENTS

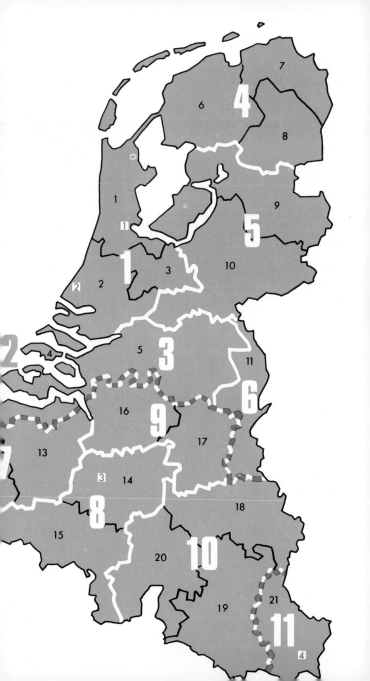

HOLLAND BELGIUM LUXEMBOURG

Their size, their adjacent location in the heart of Europe (at *the crossroads* as many say), and their intertwined history have given three separate countries one familiar name — Benelux. In fact, 'Benelux' is a customs and commercial, but not a monetary, union. It dates back to the time immediately following World War II. Together, *The Low Countries* (Belgium, Netherlands and Luxembourg), have led the way to European economic integration.

Physical boundary changes and land reclamation have altered the individual sizes of the three countries over the centuries, but even today none can be considered large. Together, Belgium which is about one fifth the size of Britain; the Netherlands, about one sixth the size of Britain; and the tiny Grand Duchy of Luxembourg, an area of 2586 sq km/999 sq mi, support a population of only some 24 million, of which the majority live in the Netherlands.

Agriculture used to be the mainstay of all three and is still important, but these days banking and finance play a major role in the economy of each, especially in Belgium and Luxembourg which have become EEC headquarters. Crafts have given way to industry of all kinds so that Holland is more famous for its electronics than diamonds, while more modern technical equipment has replaced the traditional windmill in many instances.

An American traveller might consider seeing all three countries very quickly and could not really be blamed for thinking of them as practically identical. Yet, there are some very strong contrasts, most attributable to the different national characteristics. This is very recognizable when one crosses the border from Belgium into Holland — the houses and the countryside are much neater, more compact, like the Dutch people themselves.

The Luxembourgers are a curious mixture. Stubbornly independent and loyal to their small country, they nevertheless enjoy having a good time and in this are similar to the neighbouring Belgians. Both nationalities love good food and drink, music and festivals. Both are predominantly Roman Catholic. The Dutch, on the other hand, are more solid, less volatile, and are considered the most like the British for their

tolerance and courteous manners. A large number of their population is Protestant. A typical Dutchman may have a dry sense of humour but lighter and less phlegmatic than a typical German. Although they are sometimes accused of being too reserved and standoffish, in fact they are fun-loving and friendly, always helpful. Wherever you travel in Holland, the excellent knowledge of English is bound to impress you. Like the British, the Dutch enjoy their homes and once they've decided you are a friend, will love to entertain you there. The Belgians and Luxembourgers are far more likely to invite you to join them in a restaurant. Like the French, they take more interest in how they enjoy themselves than how they live.

Even within Belgium itself, there are notable temperamental differences. The long rivalry between the French-speaking Walloons in the south (often considered more excitable and flamboyant) and the Flemings in the north (whose language, Flemish, no one but themselves seems to understand) has led to continual parliamentary debate about a split into regional government. As it stands, within this constitutional monarchy, the central government, or federal government as in the US or Germany, is in Brussels while there are separate local governments for the Walloon and Flemish areas.

Both Belgium and The Netherlands can boast seaside resorts. The West Flanders coast is Belgium's playground, its dunes and sandy beaches, its amusements and close proximity to England being the big attraction. In Scheveningen the Netherlands have a lively seaside resort right on the doorsteps of Amsterdam and The Hague. Scheveningen has now recaptured much of its former Edwardian glory after an injection of investment money. The Netherlands also have a constitutional monarchy and the governmental seat is at The Hague. The country is divided into 12

provinces, the newest of which is IJsselmeer formed through the draining of what was called the Zuider Zee. The others are Gelderland, Noord Brabant, Friesland, Overijssel, Zuid-Holland, Noord-Holland, Drenthe, Groningen, Limburg, Zeeland and Utrecht. We have divided the country into six regions of interest. They are: the northern provinces of Groningen, Friesland and Drenthe; Overijssel, Gelderland and IJsselmeer; Noord-Holland, Zuid-Holland and Utrecht; Zeeland; Noord Brabant, and Limburg.

Most of Holland is flat and much of it has been reclaimed from the sea which is why its dikes are world-famous for keeping the North Sea in its place. Because it is mostly below sea level, canals and waterways weave their way through the country. Windmills were introduced for the same reason although more modern pumping methods have taken over. Within an area of almost 42,000 sq km/16,000 sq mi there's a population of about 13,600,000, some 719,000 of whom live in the capital, Amsterdam. Among the population are Indonesians, some of whom have been born and brought up in the Netherlands, adding their own customs and spicy cuisine to the country's culture.

Despite industrial areas, Holland hangs on to its colourful traditions and dress in its small villages, and at least some of its windmills in the Kinderdijk region, where about 19 remain in operation. Holland farms its land successfully — everybody's familiar with Dutch butter and cheeses, not to mention Friesian cattle — and Dutch flowers travel all over the world.

Although many of Holland's tourist sites have been man-made, plenty remains from the Middle Ages when trade and the arts and crafts flourished. Gabled gingerbread-style merchants' houses are a much photographed feature of Amsterdam, and Rotterdam's tranquil little suburb, Delfshaven, contrasts greatly with the modern bustle of that giant port. As with England, shipping has played a vital part in Holland's past. Wedged as it is between Belgium to the south and Germany to the east, it cannot help but preserve more recent, less glorious memories of World War II. Such names as Arnhem, Nijmegen and Groesbeek are not readily forgotten.

Belgium is divided into nine provinces: Brabant (in the centre) surrounded clockwise by Antwerp, Limburg, Liège, Luxembourg (not to be confused with the neighbouring Grand Duchy of the same name), Namur, Hainaut, West Flanders and East Flanders. It is bounded to the north by Holland and the North Sea; by France to the south and by Germany to the east. We have divided the country into four regions of interest: Antwerp and Limburg in the Flemish speaking north; East and West Flanders (also Flemish); Brabant and Hainaut (centre and south-west) Liège, Luxembourg and Namur — the Ardennes.

For the most part, the northern Flemish region is flat while the ground in the south (Wallonia) is more broken. There is a high density of population in its 30,497 sq km/11,775 sq mi and a tenth of its ten million inhabitants live in the capital, Brussels. The country still has its patchworked areas of small farms and the unspoilt beauty of the Ardennes, although new towns have risen from the ravished Flanders Plain. Belgium has been the site of many battles including one of the world's most famous at Waterloo. Despite the damages of war and the mushrooming of skyscrapers, its medieval heritage is still very much intact in places like Bruges, which still looks like a town right out of the Middle Ages. Relative to its size, there are probably more churches and monasteries in Belgium than anywhere else in Europe.

Landlocked Luxembourg cannot, of course, boast of beach resorts or fishing villages, but it can boast of power. Its castles are evidence of that. The Grand Duchy is an independent sovereign state, a constitutional monarchy which is hereditary in the House of Nassau. Because of its size, we have kept it intact although administratively there are three districts: Luxembourg City, Diekirch and Grevenmacher. The executive power is in the hands of the Grand Duke and his cabinet of 11 ministers.

Although many of the people are bi- or even tri-lingual, only recently could you find a wide knowledge of English, perhaps since it has become an international financial centre. In 1955, there were only 13 banks; by the end of 1979, there were over 100. The fact that it is the second seat of the EEC is another plus factor. Per capita (and that's under 400,000) Luxembourg is one of Europe's wealthiest countries despite the fact it is dependent upon foreign trade – or perhaps because of it. Exports and imports are 80 per cent of the gross national product, compared with 50 per cent in Belgium and 20 per cent in France. Iron and steel are the main industries but viticulture is still important. Many of the country's tourists come from Belgium and Holland attracted by the forests of the Müllerthal and the rolling hills of the Oesling. (A third of the country is forested.)

Geographically, there are two distinct regions: in the north, an extension of beautiful wooded Belgian Ardennes, and in the south, soft rolling farmland with the grape-growing belt along the Moselle to the east, where it borders with Germany. The mining district is concentrated in the extreme south of the country.

A good highway system extends throughout the Netherlands and Belgium although the rules of the road are different (see p. 16). The climate in all three countries is similar and not much different from England's — reasonably temperate without extremes and summer the hottest season.

THE PAST

The first inhabitants of this area were undoubtedly the Celts. There is a recorded settlement in Belgium around AD 500 and recent archaeological excavations in Luxembourg and its surrounds has uncovered a large number of Celtic dwellings. Then came the Romans, more for trade than anything else, to be superseded by various Germanic tribes among whom the Franks were the biggest. By AD 450 they occupied the southern part of Holland, what is now Luxembourg and the greater part of what is Belgium. South of the Meuse, however, the Gallo-Roman inhabitants were left undisturbed and continued to use their own language. The linguistic boundary extended from Aachen to a point just below Brussels where it dropped down to Hazebroek in France. That line of demarcation has remained ever since, leading to the cultural and linguistic division in Belgium between the Flemings and the Walloons.

The whole of the area became part of Charlemagne's vast empire which reached its peak in 800 when Charlemagne held sway over almost the whole of Christendom, but, on his death in 814, the empire disintegrated under his weak successors and the feudal system was born. In Holland, Friesland actually managed to escape the feudal system but the rest of the country fell into semi-independent states under the rule of a variety of dukes. Belgium, too, was divided into small vassal states. At this time, Flanders and the eastern Belgian provinces went to France and the western ones to Germany. During this period, many walled towns were developed; castles and cathedrals built and trade established.

Luxembourg as a 'state' was born out of the feudal system when in 963, Siegfroid, Count of the Ardennes acquired the rocky promontory of Lucilinburhuc and built a castle. That castle was to become the centre of a fortress, city and country, and the restored remains can be seen today in Luxembourg City. For almost five centuries, first as a county, then as a duchy, it remained reasonably independent.

It was only towards the end of the 14th century that any kind of unification was achieved when the majority of the small states, including Luxembourg, were taken by force by the Dukes of Burgundy. Before that, the little state had been doing very nicely, thank you. The Countess Ermesinde in power there in the 13th century had been a good leader who succeeded in enlarging Luxembourg considerably, not by war, but through marriage alliances and purchases of land. It was her great-grandson who founded at the beginning of the 14th century a long line of counts, later dukes, who ascended the throne of the Holy Roman Empire of the Germanic nation. Among them was the popular John the Blind (who died at Crécy). His son, Emperor of Germany and King of Bohemia, conferred the status of Duchy of Luxembourg in 1354, then let his brother Wenceslas I (1353–1383) take over for what was to be a particularly prosperous period.

In 1443, Philip the Good, Duke of Burgundy conquered Luxembourg's fortress, putting an end to its independence and its links with Germany and making French the dominant language for government and administration. The last Duke of Burgundy, Charles the Bold was killed at Nancy. His daughter, Mary, saved the Low Countries and Luxembourg from being annexed to France by marrying Maximilian Habsburg of Austria.

In 1515, Charles V, Maximilian's grandson (and 'Duke of Luxembourg' since birth) joined the states of Belgium and Holland together to form the Seventeen Provinces of the Netherlands with the capital and a Royal Governor-General at Brussels. When Charles became King of Spain in 1516, it meant the whole of the Netherlands came under *Spanish Rule*. Everything remained calm (despite the effects of the Edict of Blood, 1550, which swept the rest of Europe condemning heretics to death), until Charles V resigned giving the Netherlands to his son, Philip II.

Philip II was a fanatical Roman Catholic

who set himself the task of wiping out Protestant heresy. Not surprisingly this caused the Dutch to revolt against the Spanish rule. The rule of Philip's half-sister, Margaret of Parma, proved no more palatable than that of Philip himself. A then obscure, but brilliant, nobleman, William of Nassau, Prince of Orange, supported by Counts Egmont and Horn, asked her to modify her anti-Protestant laws. When she refused, the Dutch nobility formed the *Gueux* or *Beggars Army* in 1566 which led to the 'Eighty Years' War', a series of campaigns in which both religious sides suffered. This religious split meant that in 1579 the northern provinces became the 'United Provinces of the Netherlands' while the ten southern Catholic provinces, including Luxembourg, maintained allegiance to Spain.

During Philip's reign, Portuguese ports were closed to Dutch shipping which had then to sail to Java instead of Lisbon for spices, hence the formation of the East India Company in 1602, and, in due course, the West India Company which took part in the founding of New York. With the *Treaty of Westphalia*, the Dutch won their independence from Spain in 1648 but peace eluded them for they found themselves embroiled in war with England during 1652–4 and again in 1664–7. The *Triple Alliance* (1668) of Holland, England and Sweden caused Louis XIV of France to invade Holland. In 1670, the English supported the French and it was only after some setbacks that the leader of the Dutch republic, William III, settled the troubles by marrying Mary, daughter of James II of England. However, for a brief time (1684–97) Louis XIV held Luxembourg for France. French rule was met with open arms here because, although it ended independence, the wars caused much suffering. The Duchy reverted to Spain in 1697 with the *Treaty of Ryswick*.

The *Treaty of Utrecht* in 1713 ended the War of Spanish Succession by allotting the Spanish Netherlands (Luxembourg and Belgium) to the Austrian Habsburgs. Since William III produced no heirs, however, Holland became a republic without leadership and declined in political and economic influence until it was incorporated in the French Empire in 1810. After Napoleon's defeat at Waterloo in 1815, Belgium and Holland were joined by the *Treaty of Vienna* and William of Orange was put on the throne as William I. The same treaty raised Luxembourg to the status of Grand Duchy 'to be owned in a personal capacity by the King of the Netherlands and his legitimate successors'.

William I, however, had an unhappy reign. He succeeded in being popular neither with the Belgians nor the Luxembourgers, most of whom joined the Belgians in their 1830 revolt against what they considered an artificial union. In 1831, Belgium became a separate state and Prince Léopold of Saxe-Coburg was their first elected king.

From this time on, the three countries developed separately. When William I abdicated in 1840, his son gave Luxembourg true independence from Holland so it could create its own institutions in order to reinforce the fact it was a distinct nation. In 1841, King William II granted the Grand Duchy a constitution of estates replaced in 1848 by a liberal constitution based on that of the Belgians (1830). (William II is particularly remembered for restoring independence by the equestrian statute on the Place Guillaume in Luxembourg City.)

His son, William III, delegated younger brother, Prince Henri of the Netherlands, to supervise Luxembourg's affairs. It was largely due to the latter's great sense of duty that the Grand Duchy was granted neutrality. When William III died in 1890 leaving no male heir, the dynasty of Orange-Nassau (the younger branch of the Nassau family) died out in Luxembourg. In accordance with the 1783 family pact, the successor became Adolphe of Nassau, head of the elder branch of the family, which thus created Luxembourg's own dynasty.

During World War I, the Germans occupied both Belgium and Luxembourg despite the international guarantees of neutrality, but Holland was left alone. Flanders was a continual scene of battle. After the *Treaty of Versailles*, both countries were given back their freedom. Belgium recovered from Germany the districts of Eupen, Malmédy and St Vith which were added to the province of Liège.

During World War II, all three countries were overrun by the Germans and suffered a great deal of damage. Holland was badly bombed and thousands of Dutch citizens were deported or killed, including a large Jewish community. Liberation came in May 1945. The same was true for Belgium until its liberation in 1944, while Luxembourg was the scene of heavy fighting between Americans and Germans, particularly around Wiltz and Ettelbruck, in 1944.

THE ARTS

Both the Belgians and Dutch have made many fine contributions to the arts, particularly the painters, at their peak in both countries, during the 17th century. However, the Flemish School of Art, in its early years known as the Primitives, had begun to develop in the 14th and 15th centuries. One of those noted early craftsmen was **Jan van Eyck** (1375–1441) who perfected the new oil medium and gave more realism to portraits. He became court painter to the Duke of Burgundy and settled in Bruges. Among his best works are *The Adoration of the Lamb* (an elaborate altarpiece in Ghent Cathedral) and *The Madonna of Canon van der Paele*, in Bruges Museum. Although many painters followed van Eyck's lead, one who didn't was **Hans Memling** (1430–94), a native of Germany who settled in Bruges in 1467 where many of his works may still be seen – like *The Mystical Marriage of St Catherine* in St John's Hospital.

When Bruges declined as an art centre, Antwerp took over. First of the Distinguished Antwerp painters was **Quentin Metsys** (1466–1530), some of whose pictures are in the Antwerp Museum. **Hieronymus Bosch** (1460–1516) was perhaps the greatest master of fantasy and portrayed the devilry and superstition of the Middle Ages extremely well. His *Adoration of the Shepherds* is in Brussels. In portraiture, there are many famous names: **Frans Floris** (1516–70), **Antonio Moro** (1517–76), **Pierre Pourbus** (1523–84) but the genius of **Pieter Breughel** (1525–69) is outstanding. He interpreted Flemish peasant life with an excellent satiric brush. His pictures can be seen in Brussels and Antwerp.

The zenith for Belgian painters, as mentioned, came in the 17th century, accentuated by **Pieter Paul Rubens** (1577–1640) who spent most of his life in Antwerp and died there. (His house can still be seen.) He was remarkable for his versatility not only in painting, but also in decorating, design and architecture. His style was a new one – rich, dramatic and full of colour. Antwerp houses over 20 of his major works such as *Last Communion of St Francis*, and Brussels has a fine collection including *Adoration of the Magi*.

One of the finest of Holland's early painters was **Frans Hals** (1580–1666) who painted *The Laughing Cavalier*. Born in Haarlem, he is accredited with being the founder of the Dutch School of Art. First of the so-called 'modern' painters, he specialized in civic groups and could dash off a portrait within the hour. The most famous Dutch School artist is probably **Rembrandt van Rijn** (1609–69). Born in Leiden, he came to Amsterdam to seek his fortune. In 46 years, he created 700 paintings plus hundreds of sketches and etchings. His dramatic use of light and shade is what makes *Night Watch* so celebrated (now in the Rijksmuseum). **Jan Steen** (1626–79) was a particularly

talented painter of everyday life who made his living selling beer. **Jan Vermeer** (1632–75) was another master. He used small canvases and concentrated on light, colour and texture. It was **Vincent van Gogh** (1853–90) who recaptured the magic of art. Last of Holland's great painters, he continues to be much honoured – there is a museum dedicated to his works in Amsterdam – although he spent much of his life in France. The Netherlands also gave us **Piet Mondriaan** whose abstracts influenced fashion in the 1960s.

The 13th and 14th centuries in Belgium were a peak period for silver and goldsmiths, ornate carved miniatures and wooden statuary. As elsewhere, 17th-century sculptors were influenced by the Italians. Baroque pulpits and other church furniture was made by **Cornelis Floris**, **Luc Fayd'herbe** and **Artus Quellin** and their work may be seen in several Belgian churches. Best of the modern sculptors is perhaps **Constantis Meunier** (1831–1905) whose Brussels house is a museum.

During the 15th and 16th centuries, Belgian architecture was largely dominated by the **Keldermans** family from Malines and **Van Waghemaker** of Antwerp. Their work includes Antwerp's castle, Malines Cathedral, Ghent's town hall and the wood carving on the Maison du Roi in Brussels. **Floris**, both architect and sculptor, designed Antwerp's town hall. The age of the baroque in the 17th century brought the fancy patrician homes in Antwerp and the age of Jesuit churches by **Pieter Huyssens**. Although there is less of note in the 18th century, the Cathedral of Namur designed by **Pizzoni** is worth a second glance and **Poelaert's** Palais de Justice built in Brussels between 1866 and 1883 is interesting. The art nouveau style was largely pioneered by **Victor Horta** in Brussels at the turn of the century.

Night Watch *(detail) Rembrandt*

Holland's 17th-century architecture owes much to the Flemish refugees who settled there at the time and brought their building ideas with them to be adapted to suit Holland's taste. It is not so surprising then that the Flemish style in Holland is quite similar to that in Belgium, but it is marked by higher gables with curved crow steps.

Although painting and craftsmanship were chief among the Low Countries' artistic achievements, we should note that the 16th century geographer **Mercator** (1522–94), anatomist **Vesalius** (1514–64)

Van Gogh's bedroom in Arles *Van Gogh*

and botanist **Dodoneus** (1517–85) were all born in Belgium, and that the humanist, **Erasmus** was born in Rotterdam in 1467 and lived for a while in Louvain.

Nor is music without its great names. The result of the Belgian musical movement was the setting up of two schools: that of **César Franck** (1822–90) in the Walloon region, and that of **Peter Benoit** (1834–1901) in the Flemish region. Franck began his studies in the Conservatory of Liège, his birthplace before moving to Paris. Orchestral pieces like *The Accursed Hunter* attest to his genius but he was best known as an organist. Benoit founded the Antwerp School of Music. Best appreciated are his enormous compositions like *Lucifer* and his successors have composed operas, cantatas and oratorios etc. with Dutch words. One cannot help mentioning that while Belgium has long been famous for its bells or carillons, **Adolphe Sax** (1814–94) gave a whole new direction to brass instruments by inventing the saxophone in 1846.

If you're wondering about contributions from Luxembourg, just keep on wondering. Maybe it has something to do with what Henry Miller once said: 'In Luxembourg there are no neurotic people and no lunatic asylums.' No madness – no artists!

PAPERWORK

Passports Citizens of the UK, USA or Canada require a valid passport but no visa for a visit of up to three months. For a longer duration, Americans and Canadians will need a provisional residence permit issued by the appropriate embassy or consulate in their own country. No vaccinations are necessary unless the tourist is arriving from an infected area such as Ethiopia. A British passport is obtained from The Passport Office, Clive House, Petty France, London, SW1, or from the Passport offices in Liverpool, Peterborough, Glasgow, Newport, Gwent. Two photographs are required. A British visitor's passport, valid for one year, is available from any post office. Americans can obtain passports by filing an application with any general post office, or by applying in person to The US Passport Agency in New York, Boston, Chicago, Miami, New Orleans, San Francisco, Washington or the local courthouse.

In Benelux, passports are needed for changing travellers' checks, collecting post from post offices (*poste restante*) and entrance to casinos and some private clubs.

Insurance Although the airlines automatically insure you for loss of life and/or luggage up to a certain value, it is wise to take out both travel and medical insurance before a trip. Short-term insurance is readily available through brokers or travel agencies, but major insurance companies feature policies valid by the year to cover all contingencies wherever and however often you travel abroad. If you are motoring, make sure the vehicle is insured before you depart.

CURRENCY

Both the *Luxembourg franc* (fr.) and the *Belgian franc* (fr.) have the same value. In both cases, the franc is divided into 100 *centimes*. In Belgium the smallest coin is a 50 centime piece (50 cmes) or 25 cmes in Luxembourg. Other coins come in denominations of: one, five, ten, 20 and 100 francs, but notes are more frequently used. Notes come in denominations of: 20, 50, 100, 500, 1000 and 5000 francs, except in Luxembourg where the largest note is 100 frs. Both countries' francs are legal tender in Luxembourg but not in Belgium so visitors *must* change their Luxembourg currency before leaving for Belgium. (It is possible that the Belgian province of

Luxembourg may accept money from the Grand Duchy without hassle.)

In the Netherlands, the unit of currency is the *guilder*, sometimes called a *florin* (Dfl) which is divided into 100 *cents*. Coins come in denominations of one, five, ten and 25 cents plus one and 2½ guilders. Paper money is issued in denominations of five, ten, 25, 100 and 1000 guilders.

Banks Normally, Luxembourg banks are open 0830–1230 and 1330–1630 Mon.-Fri. (Most things grind to a halt during lunch hour.) Closed Sat., and the usual bank holidays plus certain holy days such as Aug. 15 (Feast of the Assumption).

Belgian banks have increased in numbers tremendously over the last few years and there are branches of major banks throughout the country. Opening times, however, vary with location. General opening hours are: 0900–1200 and 1400–1600 Mon.-Fri. Closed weekends. Some banks do, though, stay open at midday and some stay open late on Friday or before public holidays.

Dutch banks are generally open 0900–1600 Mon.-Fri. Closed weekends and public holidays. Some banks are open in the evening.

Exchange In Luxembourg, there are few money changing offices open outside of banking hours, except at the airport and railway station. In Belgium money may be changed (including travellers' checks) at airports or official exchange offices marked *Wissel* or *Change*. These are sometimes open outside of banking hours. In Holland, money exchange offices (GWK) can be found at 28 major frontier crossings and 27 railway stations plus many KLM bus stations. Many of them are open all week and often in the evening, too. There are facilities for changing money and cashing cheques on international trains and various VVV offices (eg: in the resorts) offer change facilities.

Restrictions & Credit There are no import or export restrictions regarding money and foreign exchange for non-residents in any of the Benelux countries. Major credit cards are accepted throughout, particularly in Belgium and Holland.

HOW TO GET THERE

Air Services

UK British Airways, British Caledonian Airways, and KLM operate daily (often choice of several) scheduled service between London and Holland's international airport, Schiphol (about a 20 minute ride from Amsterdam) on a variety of fare structures. British Airways also flies direct from Birmingham and Manchester. British Caledonian serves Glasgow and Newcastle. British Island operates out of Southampton. British Midland Airways flies from the East Midlands with feeder service available from Glasgow and Belfast. Air Anglia goes from Aberdeen, Birmingham, Edinburgh, Leeds, Norwich, Teesside and Jersey. Dan-Air's routes are from Cardiff, Bristol and Teesside. KLM also serves Glasgow and Manchester. Aer Lingus services Cork, Shannon and Dublin. There are many package programmes into Holland using scheduled and charter flights.

British Airways, British Caledonian Airways and Sabena all operate frequent direct service from London to Brussels' modern international airport, Zaventem, which takes about an hour. In addition to normal first class and economy return fares, there are excursion and weekend fares available at lower prices. British Airways also operates out of Manchester; British Midland Airways offers service out of Birmingham and Air UK flies from London (Stanstead). These are all scheduled flights, some of which (along with charter flights) are used in holiday packages to Belgium. In many cases, there are several flights daily.

Luxair and British Airways fly regularly from London to Luxembourg Airport and there are connections through Brussels (in summer) or Amsterdam.

USA There is a good service to Schiphol on Pan Am and KLM, particularly from New York and Atlanta. The same holds true to Zaventem – in both cases there are holiday

packages available to the American market by tour operators featuring Europe. Air Bahamas has direct flights from the US to Luxembourg as does Icelandair out of New York and Chicago.

Canada KLM and Air Canada link Holland and Canada. Sabena and Air Canada link Belgium and Canada. There is no direct connection with Luxembourg – Canadians must travel through Brussels. Some holiday packages are available.

Sea Services

There is an excellent ferry service with several companies from England into Belgium. Passengers usually arrive at Ostend or Zeebrugge. Services operate all year round several times daily, with increased daily service in summer. As well as the regular economy fares which allow a 50 per cent reduction for children aged 4–14, there are reduced price return tickets on night returns, one day shopping trips, mini-tours etc. Tourists can choose to travel by ship, hovercraft or jetfoil.

Hoverspeed crosses the Channel from Dover to Calais and Boulogne. Sealink has the Dover/Folkestone service into Ostend and Dunkirk, Calais and Boulogne. Townsend Thorensen uses the Dover or Felixstowe-Zeebrugge route. North Sea Ferries operates Hull–Zeebrugge. The Dover–Ostend jetfoil service was introduced in 1981.

There's just as wide a choice of ferry service from England to Holland, with similar discounts and packages offered. Sealink sails from Harwich to the Hook of Holland. Norfolk Line operates from Great Yarmouth to Scheveningen; North Sea Ferries, Hull to Rotterdam; Olau from Sheerness to Vlissingen; Townsend Thorensen from Felixstowe to Rotterdam.

Car Ferries

It is easy to take your own car to either Belgium or Holland. Except for the jet-foil service, all the companies mentioned above offer car-ferry service as well as passenger service. The crossing between Dover and Ostend takes around 3¾ hours and about four hours from Folkestone. These routes could be used to get into Holland as the minimum time for a direct route (Harwich–The Hook) takes about 6½ hours.

Charges on car ferries vary with type of vehicle, sometimes number of passengers, and time of year. In most cases, fares quoted will not include berths or meals. Advance bookings are highly recommended in summer. For information on documents and regulations needed for a motoring holiday, see *If You Are Motoring*, p. 16.

Several coach companies operate from British cities (including London) directly into Belgium and Holland, but inclusive tours apart, not into Luxembourg.

Rail and Sea

There are direct rail connections from London to British ports and from Dutch or Belgian ports to the capitals or other towns. Fares will vary according to final destination. There are some links with ferries from other cities. For full information, write or telephone the shipping companies concerned (See *Useful Addresses*, p. 30) or British Rail. To Luxembourg, there is a twice-daily direct rail/sea connection from London Victoria, via Dover–Ostend. Many all-inclusive holidays feature rail and sea as the mode of transportaton.

INTERNAL TRAVEL

Domestic Flights There are no domestic flights within Belgium or Luxembourg, but in Holland, the national airline KLM operates frequent service out of Schiphol Airport (Amsterdam) to Rotterdam, Eindhoven, Maastricht, Groningen and Enschede.

Ferries In Holland, ferries link the Wadden Islands (in the north) with the rest of the country; some of the islands in the province of South Holland; and Zeeland/Flanders in the southwest. Most ferries are equipped to carry both cars and buses and fares are reasonable. Principal ferries are:
Wadden Islands: Den Helder–Texel, Harlingen–Terschelling, Holwerd–Ameland, Harlingen–Vlieland (no cars), Lauwersoog-Schiermonnikoog (no cars), **Southwest Holland**: Maassluis–Rosenburg, **Zijpe** (Schouwen–Duiveland): Zijpe–Anna Jacobapolder. **Western Scheldt**: Flushing–Breskens, Kruiningen–Perkpolder. **IJsselmeer**: Enkhuizen–Stavoren (summer only), Enkhuizen–Urk (summer only). Except for Zeeland/Flanders, Zeeland is now accessible by road from the north using tunnels, bridges and dams.

Railways The national state-owned railway in Belgium is called the *Societé Nationale des Chemins de fer Belges* (SNCB) and provides excellent service. There are two classes of travel within Belgium; first class is likely to cost 50 per cent more. An hourly service for example links Brussels with Liège (a 60 minute ride). Half hourly service links Brussels with Antwerp. Brussels to Ghent takes 30 minutes and Brussels to Bruges under an hour.

Money saving tickets are available. The *Runabout Ticket*, for example is valid over the entire network and is available in three types: five consecutive days, ten consecutive days or 15 consecutive days. There is also a Runabout Ticket valid for five days which enables the user to choose freely any five day period within a 14 day span. A *Runabout Benelux Rail-Tour* ticket allows unrestricted rail travel for ten days throughout the three countries between March and September. Available from any Benelux station.

Day return tickets are available at reduced rates throughout the year, such as 'A day at the Seaside' or 'A day in the Ardennes', whereby the tourist may choose which station he returns from. A booklet of tickets with unspecified date for day return to certain tourist centres is available at reduced cost, combined with admission price to sites of interest – *eg*: castles, museums. Destinations include Antwerp, Bruges, Dinant, Ghent and the Grottoes of Han in Luxembourg. Most of these excursions operate daily between July and August; Saturdays, Sundays and holidays as well during May, June and September.

A one month ticket allows up to 50 per cent discount on all fares. In July and August, an Excursion ticket combines rail and coach travel. NB for sports enthusiasts: many Belgian railway stations offer a bike renting service.

In Holland, modern trains operate frequent services between all points at least once an hour, and on busy routes even up to eight times an hour. Timetables are available from stations, news kiosks and bookshops. The Netherlands Railway also operates the Inter-city Network, a national system of fast trains stopping only at a few selected stations. For the same fare, you may interrupt your journey at a point of interest and continue it later in the day. Children under 4 years travel free; those 4–9 half fare for a single ticket or 40 per cent of the return. There are several discounts on a variety of return tickets, including evening or group return fares. Holland's *3–7 Day Rover* tickets are an ideal way to see some of the country. It allows unlimited travel for that period of time for one fixed price. One flat fare on a day return will allow you to travel to any Dutch destination of your choice. Ask for a *Meermanskart*, available from Netherlands Railways in the UK. Valid for 2–6 people. In addition, special tickets are available for teenagers during June, July and August.

Luxembourg's National Railways are equally efficient and punctual with frequent service to the neighbouring countries. Certain discounts are offered: *eg.* on day or weekend return tickets, *Go-as-you-Please* tickets for 1, 5 or 30 days are also available.

Buses, trams and the metro (one of Europe's most modern) serve Brussels. A flat rate fare pays for a single journey which may be a combination of all three modes of transportation. A card valid for five or ten journeys may be purchased at newspaper kiosks or metro ticket offices.

Trams and buses operate in Dutch urban areas while Amsterdam and Rotterdam additionally have a metro system. Fares differ from place to place but some transfers are available. The two major cities use zone based fares for their public transport. If you're travelling by train, at the same time buy a *National travel ticket* (four rides for a fixed price) which may be used on all local buses and trams anywhere in the country. An inter-urban network provides good service between cities and smaller places. Various bus companies offer cheap day return tickets. The VVV offices can supply you with information about price and connections.

Luxembourg has neither trams nor metro, but the local bus service is pretty good and not expensive. Cards for ten journeys may be purchased.

Taxis Belgian and Dutch taxis are very expensive since they include taxes and tips. Nor is it easy to find them cruising. They are usually ordered by telephone although there are some taxi stands. The same holds true for Luxembourg. There are few taxi stands, only at the railway station in the capital, at the Place de Paris, in the town centre on Place D'Armes, at the fish market or airport.

Excursions Organized excursions by train or boat are generally only available in the summer but local tourist offices in all three countries will tell you what tours are available through the year. Of special note are the excursions on the Meuse from Dinant in Belgium plus tours of the canals of Bruges; Rhine cruises from Rotterdam; daily coach tours from Luxembourg City, Echternach, Diekirch, Ettelbruck and Larochette; also boat trips on the Moselle.

IF YOU ARE MOTORING

Accidents in case of an accident involving injuries, in Holland call the local police number; in Belgium dial 900. In Luxembourg, call 012.

Automobile Clubs Holland has two clubs in The Hague. They are: *Koninklijke Nederlandsche Automobiel Club (KNAC), Sophialaan 4, Koninklijke Nederlandsche Toeristenbond (ANWB), Wassenaarseweg 220.* For any assistance while motoring in the Grand Duchy, contact the *Automobile Club of Luxembourg, 13 Route de Longwy, Luxembourg–Helfenterbruck (31 10 31).* Belgium has three helpful organizations: *Touring Club de Belgique, Rue Joseph 11 25, Brussels* which has local telephone numbers besides the main one – *(02 512 78 90). The Royal Automobile Club de Belgique, Rue d'Arlon 53, Brussels (02 230 0810). Vlaamse Automobilistenbond, Sint Jacobsmarkt 45, Antwerp (03 234 34 34).*

Breakdowns Any of the above will offer ready help in the case of a breakdown. Main highways in Holland are patrolled by the ANWB Wegenwacht. These expert mechanics give free service to their own members but will charge non-members for services rendered. Their vehicles and uniforms are somewhat similar to those of Britain's AA. For problems in Amsterdam, call them at 224466.

Car rental All the major rental companies have offices in all three countries (*eg.* Hertz, Avis etc.) and there are a number of local companies. The advantage of using a well-known international firm is that a car may be pre-booked and paid for at home and often has a 'pick up here, drop off there' policy. The cost of self-drive cars is similar to that in Britain and other parts of Europe and depends on size. Special rates are available with or without free mileage.

Mopeds and bikes are equally easily rented, especially in Holland and Belgium where they may be hired from railway stations as well as from dealers. Costs are inexpensive.

Essential Documents EEC nationals are required to carry only a valid driving licence and to show if necessary car registration papers. Your UK insurance policy automatically provides the minimum cover required by Benelux insurance legislation. It is recommended, however, to take out additional third party liability insurance. Canadians and Americans must have an international green insurance card. Minimum driving age is 21 in Holland, 18 in Belgium.

Fuel and oil There are two grades of fuel in all three countries. They are all well provided with service stations, often open 24 hours in the large cities. Distances aren't great so no problems should arise. Watch out, though for Sunday closures in the more remote areas such as the Ardennes or around Friesland. No concession is offered on fuel prices for foreign motorists.

Lights Dipped headlights must be used in town and on open roads while driving at night — *not* sidelights. Amber headlights are not necessary.

Offences Local police are pretty severe, though courteous, about parking, speeding and other driving offences. Providing the offence is a small one, generally an on-the-spot fine is collected. The don't drink-and-drive laws are applicable to all three countries.

Seat Belts When a car is fitted with seat belts, they must be worn by people sitting in the front. If there is room in the back, children under 12 are not allowed to use the front seat. You are required to carry a red **warning triangle** with you in case of a breakdown in which case it must be placed 30m/98ft behind the vehicle in the direction of the traffic endangered by it. **Horns** may not be used in traffic congestion except when a dangerous situation is imminent.

Where there are **specific cycle tracks**, cyclists and moped riders must keep to them. (They are shown by a round blue sign with a white bicycle on it.) It is also compulsory for both rider and pillion passenger to wear a **crash helmet** when riding a motor bike or moped with a maximum speed more than 20 kph/13 mph.

Roads Holland's road system is an excellent one that includes major two and three-lane highways. Even small country roads are in top condition. All the Dutch signposts have blue and white striped posts. Belgium's roads have greatly improved over the last few years and the network is one of Europe's densest. Motorways cover most of the country, except the Ardennes and access is free. Luxembourg has many country roads as well as a dense network of motorways.

Motorways into European countries are marked green and have the symbol 'E' on them. National motorways are marked red with the symbol 'A'. Roads in all three countries use the European numbering system.

Rules of the Road Cars drive on the right, overtaking on the left. Police cars, fire engines and trams all have priority and at junctions, it is the cars coming from the

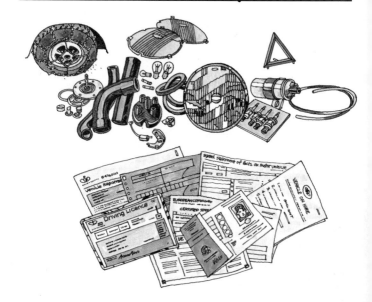

right which have the priority unless shown otherwise. Priority road traffic has priority over that from side streets; fast moving over slow; and traffic continuing straight ahead, over that turning right.

Road signs Priority roads are marked by diamond-shaped orange signs edged in white while priority crossings have the internationally used red triangle containing a thick black arrow with a thin transverse line on a white background. In Holland's built-up areas, you will see a blue sign with a white house on it which means children may be playing in the street. Pedestrians have the right of way, slow traffic coming from the right has priority and parking may only be done in zones marked 'P'.

Speed Limits/Parking Belgium and Luxembourg have the same speed limits: for cars travelling in towns, 60 kph/37mph; outside built up areas, 90 kph/55mph and 120 kph/75 mph on motorways. The **minimum** motorway speed is 70 kph/45 mph. For some reason, Holland's speed restrictions differ slightly: in towns it is 50 kph/30 mph; outside built up areas, 100 kph/60 mph including motorways.

Parking and stopping are forbidden on pavements, footpaths or cycle tracks; on pedestrian crossings or at bus stops; on entry and exit lanes at road junctions. You may not stop at any time on a main road or motorway unless in an emergency, and then use the hard shoulder. Nor can a vehicle be left too near a corner at a junction, where there is a 'no parking' sign, or anywhere that would obstruct other road users' view of a traffic light, traffic or directional sign.

ACCOMMODATION

Hotels/Inns There is no official classification of hotels within Belgium although cities like Brussels have their own voluntary classification. Nevertheless, there are basically four categories: luxury, first class, second class and third class. Accommodations may also be called an *auberge, hostellerie* or *gasthof* in which case it will be more like the equivalent of a one or two-star country hotel or inn. Whatever they are, all those recognized by the Belgian authorities must hang a sign outside and post their rates at reception and in the rooms.

In the luxury category, you can expect the kind of facilities you'd find in a top city hotel: rooms with bath and television, air conditioning and telephone; choice of bars and restaurants; spacious public areas and shopping arcade plus function rooms for seminars and conferences. The majority of such hotels are to be found in Brussels, which has its fair share of well-known international hotel chain names such as Hilton and Holiday Inn. Most of them serve an international cuisine, accept major credit cards and may be booked through their British and/or American offices or representatives. Rates are usually quoted on an EP (room only) plan. All hotel rates are inclusive of 16 per cent service charge. A few, like the Arcades Stephanie or the Novotel, have their own swimming pool.

The hotels and inns in a lower category obviously feature fewer facilities though not necessarily less comfort. Those in small towns may be family run – you'll eat in the cafe/bar and rates are more often on a bed and breakfast or MAP (breakfast and one other meal) basis. Usually, full pension (full board) can be negotiated for a minimum of three days. The smaller the establishment, the more likelihood of country cooking. All room rates include a 16 per cent service charge, as a general rule. Children are particularly welcome in Belgian hotels, many of which offer special prices for them.

Dutch hotels and motels are among the cleanest and most comfortable in Europe, however modest they might be and in whatever location. Courteous, efficient service is a Dutch trademark and the wide knowledge of English is a plus factor. Hotels are graded on a (voluntary) star system, highest of which is a 4 star and in descending order, 3, 2, 1A and 1. There are good hotels in all of Holland's major cities and towns, varying in style from a converted mansion, a gracious old hotel like the Amstel in Amsterdam to modern blocks with the international names like Hilton or Howard Johnson. As a rule, 15 per cent service charge is included in the room rate, which as in Belgium is controlled and has to be posted. Rates often include breakfast.

The official Dutch Tourist Organisation (its information offices are known by the initials VVV) publishes a useful guide called *Hotels in Holland* which can be obtained at its local offices or offices abroad. Free reservations for hotels in all price brackets may be made through Holland's National Reservations Centre, POB 404, 2260 KA Leidschendam. (070 202 500). Accommodation will be reserved and confirmed for the price of a phone call, telex or stamp.

Luxembourg, which used to have no really grand de luxe hotels, now has two new 5 star city hotels: Le Royal and an Inter-continental. The only familiar chain name is Sheraton which runs the Aerogolf, one of the capital's best hotels. Outside of Luxembourg City, there are few big hotels. A 15 per cent service charge is added to the bill. Room rates often include breakfast in the large towns and in the country, half or full board.

Boarding/Guest Houses You can find this family-style accommodation throughout the three countries in a much lower price range than the hotels or motels. In Belgium and Luxembourg they're likely to be called a *pension*. Some will only offer bed and breakfast and some (in the villages) will offer full board. In either case, the rate will be set and you won't be able to change it.

All recognized *pensions* must display a sign and should be booked in advance, certainly during the tourist season. Peak months throughout the Low Countries are July and August. Holiday periods such as Easter, Whitsun and Christmas are also heavily booked. In Holland, bulb time (April/May) is considered high season as well, so book as much in advance as possible.

Villas/flats Self-catering accommodation has flourished over the last few years. Most of Belgium's flats and bungalows to let are found in the coastal regions and Ardennes. They are very self-contained and comfortably furnished although you will need to bring bedclothes, table linen and sometimes cutlery with you. Rented premises usually comprise living room, kitchen and one or more bedrooms.

You can find holiday accommodation by contacting one of the real estate agents in the coastal areas or tourist information offices in the Ardennes region. If you're dealing with an estate agent, make sure you state the type of accommodation you're seeking, location (seafront or residential, etc.), comfort required and price. About 10–20 per cent of the rent is generally demanded as security and will not be refunded until a few months after your departure so that any expenses incurred and left unpaid may be deducted from it. Although some agents will let for a week, in July and August, a two-week rental is the usual minimum. It is a good idea to see what you're renting in advance so perhaps take a winter weekend.

For information about the coast, contact: Chamber of Real Estate Agents Association of the Belgian Coast, Christinastraat 61, 8400 Ostend. For a listing of 750 furnished residences in the Ardennes, write: Fédération Touristique du Luxembourg Belge, Quai de L'Ourthe 9, 6980 La Roche-en-Ardenne. (Use an international reply coupon.)

Holland has what it calls 'holiday chalets' — family style accommodation in bungalows or cottages or chalet units. These are to be found in some 500 parks and advance reservations are essential (even earlier than for boarding houses). The Provinciale VVV Zeeland, POB 123 Middelburg. (01180 28051); the VVV Texel POB 3, Den Burg. (02220 2844) operate a centre for the rental of holiday facilities in their area.

There are some holiday flats available in Luxembourg. The Luxembourg National Tourist Office, 36/37 Piccadilly, London W1 (01 434 2800) publishes a free pamphlet giving information as to their location and facilities.

Farms Farming holidays are so popular that the number of rooms available is limited. In Belgium the majority are found in the Ardennes although there are some in West Flanders. In Holland, there are a few in Gelderland. (See *Useful Addresses*, p. 29).

Camping Campsites in all three countries are plentiful. In Belgium there are over 500 registered campsites in four categories. The majority are in the Ardennes or on the coast. The 4-star sites have electrical facilities throughout, restaurant, children's play area and sports ground in addition to day and night surveillance, lit pathways and warm-water showers found at the 3-star sites. In a 1-star site you can only expect cold water showers. Each item is priced separately (number of adults and children, car, caravan or tent space). Charges are reasonable, although a 25 per cent summer supplement is added on the coast.

Holland has about 2000 campsites which have been vetted for quality of standard and space. The amount of equipment provided varies considerably from site to site beyond the basic essentials. Some sites charge from midnight to midnight to encourage longer stays. An overall space fee is charged per night for four people, tent or caravan and car. Local VVVs have lists of campsites in their areas, but cannot make reservations for you. In all cases, these must be made direct.

Camp grounds in three categories, with different amenities may also be found throughout Luxembourg.

Youth Hostels There are innumerable hostels in all three countries. A number of youth advisory centres have been set up in Belgium to help young people to find cheap lodging and meals and introduce them to other associations. You can obtain a complete list of Belgian youth hostels from the Belgian National Tourist Office or write for information to: Infor-Jeunes, Rue Marché aux Herbes 27, 1000 Brussels, or Info-Jeugd, Gretry-straat 28, 1000 Brussels.

Holland's 52 youth hostels of the Stichting Nederlandse Jeugdherberg Centrale (NJHC), Prof. Tulpplein 4, 1018 GX, Amsterdam (020 264433) are open all year to anyone who is a member of a youth hostel organization in their own country or who holds an international youth hostel card (true for all Benelux). In some hostels there is a kitchen for self-catering.

In Luxembourg young people under 18 may stay without a membership card if they are accompanied by an adult who does possess one. In addition to hostels, there are rest houses (*gîtes d'ètape*) which do not require youth organization membership but do not accommodate both sexes. There's a fixed nightly charge. For information, write: Gites d'Etape Luxembourgeois, Wiltz 10, Rue des Tanneurs. (9 50 22).

FOOD AND DRINK

If lingering three hours over a meal is your idea of a good time, Belgium is the place. The Belgians are hearty eaters, even around midday. Restaurants serve first class food but their fare tends to be richer, heavier and less sophisticated than the French. The accent is on quantity which means you may find eating places serving 'second helpings' as a matter of course. Soups are abnormally thick. Meats are often braised in beer. Favourite starters include a wide variety of pâtés or sausages. Dishes are often interesting combinations with fruit which grows in plenty in Belgium. And sweets are creamy, nutty, filling – and oh so calorific!

An English-style breakfast is, of course, always available at the top hotels, but the usual Belgian breakfast is continental-style with perhaps the addition of ham or other cold meats and cheese. Lunch is generally quite a full meal although dinner is the main meal of the day. I like the typical old-style Belgian restaurants which often have wood or mirrored walls, a coffee-house style of table and bench seating, and are brightly lit. If you want cheap, fast food, look out for *fritures* or *snackbars*.

In general, mealtimes are: 0600–0930 (breakfast); 1200–1400 (lunch) and 1800–2200 (dinner). It is Belgian law that all restaurants must display their menu outside. Quite often they feature fixed-price meals. Many prices are quoted *all inclusive* (including tax and service), but even so, it is courtesy to leave the waiter any small change. If prices are not inclusive, it is customary to give a 16 per cent tip. Except for the fast food outlets, restaurants are not cheap.

Pâté is one of the most popular starters in Belgium, made with cream, pepper, game (particularly woodcock). A very fine pâté is called a *mousse*. A favourite soup is made from chervil and leek, mixed with celery, asparagus and other vegetables. Or try chicken livers on toast as an appetizer.

Beef in Belgium is good and most usually cooked rare unless you specify otherwise. Lamb is mostly imported and generally cooked with garlic – saddle and leg are the most popular cuts. Pork is considered a cheap meat. Quite often Ardennes ham is served as a main course, as are *boudin blanc* and *boudin noir* (local sausages). An *assiette Anglaise* (English plate) comprises cold meats and salad. In winter, game is the favoured main course such as saddle of hare or wild boar. Fresh seafood in the coastal regions is often cooked with fennel and the Dutch herring in season (*maatje* or raw

herring) is just as popular in Belgium. Mussels (*moules*) are another Belgian favourite, especially around the Rue des Bouchers in Brussels, where the restaurants serve them in huge, steaming platefuls, accompanied by *frites*.

One of the country's national dishes is *carbonnade flamande* (beef cooked in beer). On a tourist menu, only potatoes will accompany the entrée and they're likely to be French fries which are delicious and are served with everything.

Vegetables are likely to be served with a sauce, or as a mixture. For example, in spring, try fresh *asparagus à la flamande* (dipped in a sauce made from hard boiled eggs, butter and parsley). Asparagus with leeks and ham may be served in a cheese sauce. Red cabbage often turns up mixed with apples, as does chicory. In a really good restaurant don't be surprised to find hop shoots a delicacy. They can only be found at the beginning of the growing season and, like tiny asparagus, have their own distinctive flavour. When beans are served, they are almost always small, like flageolets.

A wide variety of tarts will be found on dessert trolleys. They could include *tarte au maton* with cheese curd filling, *tarte au flan* with baked custard or *tarte au riz* (rice tart). And special cakes are made for special occasions during the year. Waffles and crêpes are common.

Belgium doesn't produce any wine of its own, but French and Luxembourg wines are readily available and not expensive. Beer is produced locally and is probably the country's national drink. *Export* is the most popular brand. *Geuze* is a rich bottled beer and *Lambic* is like draught. Louvain's *Artois* beer is very well known and the brewery is Belgium's largest.

The country's licensing laws, however, are somewhat complex. While you can take a *porto* (a light red or white port) in a cafe, you cannot drink spirits unless you're in a private club. This simply means that a number of cafes and drinking establishments have become 'private clubs' and you're an instant 'member' – *eg*, at hotels – so really, tourists aren't affected.

It has been said of Luxembourg that its cuisine is characterized by the quality of the French and the quantity of the German. Happily indeed, it inherits the best of both. In some ways, it is similar to that of Belgium – often rich, with a cream and butter basis and, like Belgium, Luxembourg produces some excellent *charcuterie*. Ardennes ham, here, too, is a favourite, smoked over wood and served with herbs, or cut paper thin and served raw. Then there's a good choice of pâtés like *pâté au riesling* (a speciality made with wine), sausages and black puddings.

Beef and lamb are rather expensive but local chefs are wizards with pork. The French undoubtedly left their mark with their sauces, quite often served with meats (generally veal or pork). Look for *judd mat gardebohn'en* (smoked neck of pork served with broad beans in a cream sauce). Restaurants along the Moselle River serve pike in a cream sauce. Fresh water fish such as pike or trout, in fact, are served in a variety of ways. Venison appears on menus frequently and the German influence is felt with *quenelles* of calves' liver served with sauerkraut – or suckling pig. If you're up to it, try the local cheese called *kachkés* which is 'cooked in the making'. Strongly flavoured, it's a bit gluey, but good when served on bread with a liberal dose of mustard.

Most of Luxembourg's restaurants are rustic. Menu prices generally include tax and service, but an additional 10 per cent tip is nevertheless expected. Large restaurants give German and English translations from the French, but in the smaller places, you may have to brush up on *le français*. An average three course meal is usually modestly priced but be prepared to pay considerably over the odds for one that isn't that lavish.

If the Luxembourgers are good eaters, they are more than certainly good drinkers. Not only do they produce and drink their own white wines and champagnes, but they also import them from France. The local wines are less sweet than the German ones and are cheap to buy in supermarkets or restaurants. Brewing is also a traditional industry in the Grand Duchy. Well known brands are: *Funck, Mousel, Clausen* and *Diekirch*.

Local liqueurs of all kinds are available, often made in illegal stills. The ones you know you can obtain include a delicious *framboise* (strawberry juice with a kick!), *mirabelle*, made from wild cherries, *prunelle* and *quetsch*, both plum-based. Varieties of mineral water are plentiful, as is grape juice.

Although I can't promise that Dutch food is on the same level, the Dutch, too, eat well. It is true that eating out in Holland isn't quite as exciting as dishes tend to be plain rather than imaginative, but they are good. Perhaps it is the Dutch practicality that makes breakfast the large meal it is. Eggs and bacon may not be their national dish, but the Dutch continental spread has lots of cold meats, cheeses, breads and sometimes boiled eggs along with coffee, tea or chocolate.

The average lunch is a light one, known as a *koffietafel* (literally translated as coffee table), almost a repeat of breakfast although salad is included and, in cold weather, often a hot dish. Dinner is the main meal of the day, although taken fairly early between 1800 and 2000. The Dutch are fond of soups, particularly heavy soups, like pea with pork or *erwtensoep*, especially in winter. Another soup to look for is *groentensoep*, a clear consommé filled with vegetables, vermicelli, tiny meatballs and spiced with mace. Stews like *hutspot*, made with beef, onions, mashed potatoes and carrots, are a mainstay. The Dutch are very fond of mashing vegetables and potatoes together. Other mixtures you'll find are sauerkraut with bacon or curly kale with sausage.

Meat is all high quality and asparagus just one of the much loved side dishes. (The large white kind is available in May/June.) Seasonal seafood is typically Dutch: oysters and mussels between September and March; salted raw herring during the first few weeks of May when they are sold *green* or as *new herring* right off roadside stands, and eaten on the spot.

Holland's fruits are excellent and the Dutch adore whipped cream (*slagroom*) on everything. Try *flensjes* or *pannekoeken* (pancakes) with or without the cream. (There are savoury ones as well – *eg:* bacon with apple). Look out for *poffertjes*, small lumps of dough dusted with icing sugar and fried. You may well prefer the cheeseboard to dessert – if you have managed to evade it in the other courses (cheese finds its way into soups, soufflés, sauces and croquettes). The Dutch prefer cheese as a snack or with an aperitif than following a meal. Some 26 varieties are produced including dessert cheeses like soft *kernhem*.

Eating out in Holland need not be pricey. There are loads of *broodjeswinkels* (sandwich shops) where you can buy *broodjes* filled with a variety of mixtures like smoked eel, tuna, liverworst. A light lunch might compromise an *uitsmijter* (which means 'bouncer') – two slices of bread with ham, roast beef or cheese topped by two or three fried eggs. Or look for restaurants posting a *tourist menu* sign outside – the VVV (Dutch Tourist Information office) recognizes some 700 throughout the country which have been personally checked and many feature special children's menus.

The Dutch are keen on snacks – mid morning, tea time or *borrel* time, around 1700. Pubs and cafes are social rendezvous for a glass of *genever* perhaps, the national drink. That's a gin, but more viscous and sweeter than the gins we're used to. Normally, it is drunk without a mixer, but always well chilled. Different varieties include: *jonge* (young) containing less sugar than *oude* (old) or made with fruit like *bessenjenever* (redcurrant gin) or *citroenjenever* (lemon gin).

As the Dutch have such a sweet tooth, they produce many liqueurs, and have done since the 17th century. The choice in the bodegas or taverns is large, prices are low. Try *kummel*, flavoured with caraway seeds, which is less sweet than *curaçao*, named after the island in the Dutch West Indies, with its taste of orange, or *triple sec*, similar to cointreau. *Bols* and *De Kuyper* are both well-known brands.

Like Belgium, Holland produces no wines but the Dutch are certainly skilled brewers. *Pils* and *Amstel* are among the best – good accompaniments for a *rijsttafel* (rice table) which came about through Indonesian trade. It comprises some 15–50 *sambals* or side dishes of spicy delicacies to go with the rice. Favourites include *loempia* (a kind of egg roll) and *saté* (charcoal grilled meat cubes with a peanut sauce). In the small cafes selling Indonesian noodle-based dishes like *bami goreng* or *nasi goreng*, the Dutch often add their own particular touches – a fried egg on top or ham or pork underneath.

ENJOY YOURSELF

Cruising Holland has more than 1000 lakes and 3220km/2000mi of canals and waterways so boating of all kinds is popular. Cruising is somewhat restricted to the deep lakes. Bear in mind that the maximum draft for inland lakes is about 1.25m/4ft and for the IJsselmeer, 1.60m/5¼ft. Organized boat tours can be made over the Frisian Lakes and those in the province of South Holland; down the Rhine; round Rotterdam's harbour; through Amsterdam's canals, and many more.

Caves Belgium has some magnificent caves, especially in the Ardennes. The grottoes in Dinant are a big attraction – the cavern is enormous. The Grottoes of Han feature a subterranean lake. The River Lesse has created underground caves at Rochefort of cathedral-like proportions, also noted for their multi-coloured rock formations. Comblain-au-Pont, Petigny grottoes of Neptune and Goyet all have caverns of great interest to tourists. There are also some interesting caves in the Ardennes region of Luxembourg.

Cycling Bike rental is easily available

throughout and in certain centres there are specific cycle routes. Belgium encourages cyclists by renting bikes at many train stations for a small charge per day. The Dutch are a nation of cyclists so you'll find a highly developed system of cycle tracks and trails throughout the country. Bikes (and mopeds) may be rented from many dealers and repair shops, and at a large number of train stations. Ask for the **Rijwielstalling** at the latter. Produce a railway ticket and the hire charge is lower. You'll need some proof of identity and may have to give a deposit. In Luxembourg, there is a cycle track from Diekirch to Echternach for a distance of 30km/19mi and Vianden. The **Triangle Cyclotouriste**, a circuit of 274.4km/171.5mi, is organized all year round for biking enthusiasts who are not members of a club. Write: 16 Rue Emile Mayrisch, Soleuvre, for more information. There are also tracks from Luxembourg–Diekirch and Luxembourg–Hespérange.

Fishing Anglers can take their pick in Belgium from innumerable spots. Sea fishing is very popular and is good from Ostend, Nieuwpoort and Zeebrugge. Along the Belgian coast there are plenty of jetties and piers from which to fish. In addition to those mentioned, Blankenberge also has a suitable pier and breakwaters. The rivers in the Ardennes are other good areas for pike, carp and trout. A fishing licence is necessary and costs vary as there are three types, depending upon where you plan to fish. Licences are valid for a year and available from any Belgian post office. There are some closed seasons for certain fish. Anglers should check with the nearest Office of Tourism in the area.

Sea fishing in the north of Holland is good around Zeeland's harbours and no permit is required. Fishing in the Netherlands generally means coarse fishing. There are plenty of places to choose from including the Loosdrecht Lake in Utrecht, the Nieuwkoop Lakes in Zuid-Holland or the district around Schagen and Kolhoorn in Noord-Holland. A fishing licence is needed for inland waters and there are some closed seasons, and restrictions on the size of fish you catch. For general information, contact: Nederlandse Vereniging van Sportvissersfederaties (NVVS), Van Persijnstraat 25, POB 288, Amersfoort. (033 34924) or The Algemene Hengelaarsbond (General Anglers' Association), Weteringschans 106, Amsterdam 2 (020 62874) for information on gear, fishing waters and permits etc. (Licences are available from post offices.)

Luxembourg's many rivers provide a number of fishing possibilities – a monthlong tourist licence to fish the lake of the barrage of the Upper Sûre and from the banks of the Middle Sûre can be quite expensive, but on other inland rivers, a licence may only cost half as much. You will need written consent from the tenant of the fishing rights (they are all leased). This is also true for fishing along the Our, but no permit is required. Details may be checked with Administration des Eaux et Forêts, POB 411, Luxembourg.

Golf In Belgium, there are golf courses at Antwerp (Kapellenbos), Brussels (Tervuren), Dinant (Houyet), Ghent (Sint-Martens-Latem), Grez-Doiceau, Houthalen, Keerbergen, Knokke-Heist (where there are two), Liège (Sart-Tilman), Mons (Erbisoeul), Ostend (Klemskerke) and Spa. Holland has 26 courses open to members of foreign clubs including 18-hole ones at Duivendrecht, near Amsterdam and Wassenaar near The Hague. More information from Nederlandsche Golf Comite, van Alkemadelaan 676, The Hague. (070 240698), or the Nederlandse Golf Federatie, Soestdijkerstraatweg 172, Hilversum (035 830565), which organises all national and international golf tournaments. Luxembourg only has one course 7km/5mi away from the capital but it is a difficult one. Open only to members of foreign clubs.

Hunting You need to be in touch with licence holders or owners of shooting grounds. There are stag and wild boar in the Ardennes region and the Belgian huntsman can obtain a five-day licence for foreign guests. The Royal St Hubert Club, 1 Place Jean Jacobs, Brussels 1000 can help you make arrangements. In Holland, the host must apply for a six-day licence. Hunting season runs August/September until January/February, but is not allowed on Sundays. No restrictions on importing shotguns. Contact the Koningklijke Nederlandse Jagersvereniging, Utrechtseweg 131, 3818 ED Amersfoort (033 19841). In Luxembourg local hunters must apply for a one or five-day visitor permit for guests.

Riding A number of riding stables are located on the Belgian coast with horses for hire and sometimes lessons given. Rides from 2–12 days can be organized through the country. For information on riding events, write to: Federation Belge des Sports Equestres, avenue Hamoir 38, 1180 Bruxelles. (02 374 47 34). Racing enthusiasts will find courses at Ostend (the Wellington Hippodrome, summer); Boitsfort (Groenendael course); Sterrebeek (trotting) and Waregem (steeplechase, end of August). There are several riding schools in Holland and a number of hotels operate stables of their own. International show jumping takes place in Amsterdam, Geersteren, Den Bosch, Leeuwarden, Rotterdam and Zuidlaren. Further details may be obtained from the Stichting Nederlandse

Hippische Sportbond, POB 97639, 2509 GA Den Haag. (070 245 484). Trotting and flat racing takes place at Duindigt in The Hague and in Emmeloord at regular intervals, among other places. Luxembourg, too has a few riding schools. Contact the Sécretariat de la Fédération Luxembourgeoise des Sports Equestres, 90 Route de Thionville, Luxembourg, which also organizes riding tours.

Sailing/Boating Belgium's lakes are suitable for sailing or rowing and its rivers for canoeing; its coastal areas for boating of all kinds. Sand yachting is popular on the west coast and is practised on beaches from Oostduinkerke to De Panne. In Holland, the best lakes for sailing include those in Friesland, western Holland and Zeeland plus those 'encircled' by Utrecht, Bussum, Haarlem and Leiden. The choice is really a large one. Most accessible to Amsterdam are Kagerplassen, Brasemermeer, Westeinder Plas and Loosdrechtse Plassen. No certificate for yachts or motorboats is needed but a permit may be required for certain waterways. Sailing regattas and boat races are frequently held at centres like Loosdrecht (at Easter), Warmond (July), Enkhuizen (July/August) and Sneek (August). Charts of lakes and waterways may be obtained from the Royal Dutch Touring Club (ANWB) whose head office is at Wassenaarseweg 220, The Hague or at any of their 23 branches. Other details from the Cruising Office, Museumplien 5, Amsterdam, or any VVV office.

In Luxembourg serious boating can be done on the Moselle and Lower Sûre and also on the Clerve, Wiltz, Our and Upper Sûre, for fun boating. There are some restrictions in places. Check with the Fédération Luxembourgeoise de Canoe-Kayak, POB 424, Luxembourg.

Skating Holland has 21 skating rinks including those at The Hague, Amsterdam, Deventer and Tilburg which also hold ice hockey matches and ice shows. Skating tours and races are organized over various distances on a number of frozen canals in winter such as the Molen and Plassentochten. Top international event when conditions are suitable is the Eleven Towns Race held over 201km/125mi of waterway in Friesland. The Royal Netherlands Skaters' Association, Stadsring 103, 3811 HP Amersfoort. (033 30491).

Skiing Belgium's Liège province has several winter resorts. Snow is usually plentiful from October to March at Bütgenbach, Jalhay, Francorchamps, Robertville-Ovifat, Beverçé-Malmédy, Eupen, Trois-Ponts and Spa. Equipment may be hired at most centres. Contact the Tourist Federation of Liège, 77 Boulevard de la Sauvenière, 4000 Liège (041 22 42 10).

Swimming/Water skiing/Sub Aqua Endless possibilities to swim, ski and dive in the lakes and rivers of all three countries and the coasts of Holland and Belgium. In Holland, best seaside resorts are Scheveningen, Noordwijk aan Zee and Zandvoort. In Belgium, the Flanders shores boast lively resorts like Ostend. In Luxembourg, the lake of the Upper Sûre is the most popular recreational area. The Nederlandse Onderwatersportbond, Nassaustraat 12, 3583 XG Utrecht, will advise on underwater sports in Holland. Luxembourg's Sub Aqua Club has an equipped base at the Upper Sûre lake, open to anyone interested on Sundays and holidays from 1 May to 31 October.

Tennis Public tennis courts are plentiful throughout the Low Countries. Additionally, many hotels in resort locations have their own courts.

Walking/Climbing Rock climbing may be done on the cliffs along the banks of the Meuse in Belgium as well as the Ourthe, the Molignée and the Samson. The Belgian Alpine Club, Rue de l'Aurore 19, 1050 Brussels, (02 648 86 11) has a school at Freyr.

Well-marked walking paths and trails can be found throughout the area, it is such a popular pastime. All year round, Holland's walking sports association organizes tours including: Duinenmars (April) in The Hague, Rosamars in Nijmegen (April or September), South Limburg three day round-trip (May/June) and Amersfoort two-day tour (end of June). Information from NWB Rubenslaan 123, Utrecht, (030 517389) and the KNBL, Valkenbosplein 18, The Hague (070 458573). Luxembourg's network of marked walking paths is the densest in the world. National routes (15) range from 13km/8mi to 67km/42mi in length. Organized walking tours take place practically every Saturday, Sunday or holiday on marked circuits 10km/6mi to 40km/25mi for a small fee. Information from Fédération Luxembourgeoise des Marches Populaires, 13 Rue Lohr, Mersch.

War Graves and Memorials Throughout Belgium and in parts of Holland and Luxembourg there are cemeteries and memorials to those who died in the two World Wars. For further information contact The Commonwealth War Graves Commission, 2 Marlow Road, Maidenhead, Berks (0628 34221); The American Battle Monuments Commission, 4C014, Forrrestal Buildings, 1000 Independence Avenue, SW, Washington, D.C. 20314 (202 693 6067/6089) or 68, Rue du 19 Janvier, 92-Garches, France (1 970 01 73/20 70). Inquirers seeking a particular grave should provide the full name and any service details known of the deceased.

ENTERTAINMENT

When it comes to a lively nightlife, the Netherlands is undoubtedly the best prepared and best known. Certainly Amsterdam has a reputation for 'fun living' for the Dutch tolerance has allowed the city an 'anything goes' attitude. This means there's evening entertainment to suit all tastes. The notorious 'Red Light District' (where the girls sit in their windows to await customers) not only attracts clients, but voyeurs as well. The city has more than its fair share of gay bars, sex shows and striptease, but it also can boast good cabaret clubs, discotheques and dance spots.

Basically, the capital has three nightlife areas, the oldest of which is the sailors' quarter, the Nieuwendijk-Zeedijk. The Rembrandtsplein and adjacent Thorbeckeplein are both squares encompassed by all kinds of nightclubs – the latter is especially lively. The newest district is around Leidesplein with lots of bars and beat music. All the top hotels offer live music, disco or other kinds of entertainment.

Don't expect to find neon in Holland's small villages, but the seaside resorts like Scheveningen, Zandvoort and Noordwijk have lots happening in a variety of price ranges in season. Other cities with good nightlife include The Hague and Rotterdam. Some nightspots with floor shows have an international programme. Expect to pay an entrance fee at all the better establishments. Most remain open until around 0400.

Gambling is legal in Holland. Casinos featuring roulette and blackjack may be found in Zandvoort, Valkenburg and Scheveningen. Open all year from 1400-0200. Players must be over the age of 18.

All of Holland's cities have first class theatres, cinemas and concert halls. The annual Holland Festival (June 1–23) comprises concerts, opera, chamber music and ballet in several centres including Amsterdam, The Hague, Rotterdam and Utrecht. Cinemas show films in their original language, subtitled in Dutch.

Fairs and festivals take place in a variety of towns at varying times of the year. Many have something to do with Holland's famous flowers – like the September *Bloemencorso* in Aalsmeer – or its cheeses. Christmas is celebrated with great verve all over. Marzipan, in all shapes and forms, fills the shops and *speculaas* (spiced ginger biscuits) or *taai-taai* (spiced cake) is sold in the form of animals or figures.

At first glance, Belgium doesn't appear to be a very swinging place after dark, but because it is a 'club town' (See *Food and Drink*, pp. 20–3), there's a lot more than the eye can see, especially in Brussels, which on the face of it appears to be quiet and reserved. There are private strip, gambling, even slightly orgiastic clubs in the major cities – if you know where to find them. Make a friend and take along your passport.

There are several easily found nightspots featuring live cabaret in Brussels, the best known of which is *Show Point*. International performers also appear at *Chez Paul au Gaity*. Besides the capital, Antwerp and Liège have a reasonable number of nightclubs and discotheques or variety shows. Ghent has some as well. Most top hotels have dine and dance restaurants.

There are cinemas throughout Belgium but in the Walloon area, they're liable to be dubbed in French. On the coast and throughout Flanders, dubbing is mainly English. Good theatre, opera and ballet can be found in every large city. Belgium is especially noted for its puppet theatres which you can find in Bruges, Brussels, Antwerp, Ghent, Liège and Mechelen, among others. Casinos are open year round at Ostend, Blankenberge, Knokke-Heist, Middelkerke, Namur, Spa, Dinant and Chaudfontaine.

Belgium probably has more festivals than anywhere else in Europe. One of the biggest is the *Festival of Flanders*, one of Europe's most important music festivals. The April, May and June portion of this includes orchestral concerts in Antwerp, choirs in Kortrijk, sacred music near Tongeren and concerts in the château near Sint-Truiden. The summer section involves a variety of musical events between 1 August and 30 September. Principal festival centres are Ghent, Brussels and Leuven.

Carnival season is celebrated vigorously by all of Belgium. The origins of the Aalst procession go back 500 years. This one has acquired international fame, but others worth noting are in Blankenberge, Bruges, Genk, Hamont and Knokke-Heist. The carnival at Malmedy is very interesting and attracts large crowds. There are so many processions that they have to be divided between all the Sundays in Lent. One you'll hear a lot about in eastern Belgium is a *Rosenmontag*, the most characteristic of which is held at Eupen.

You can see folk dancing in a number of towns. Middelkerke's international festival takes place over two weekends in July which is also the month for Schoten's. Jambes holds its folk festival on an August weekend. Celebrations dedicated to harvest time, fishermen and religious ideals are other events.

Luxembourg is fairly enmeshed in folklore, too, although most of this tiny country's annual fairs revolve around the wine producing region. Spring and autumn are the two best times of the year to join in the merrymaking in towns and villages along the Moselle, when there is wine tasting, fireworks and dancing in the streets.

Nightlife *per se* can't be considered sophisticated. Only in the capital can you find proper nightclubs with floorshows, like the *Splendid*, or discotheques. Most of the other tourist centres are little more than villages and the pavements roll up early. Along with the spa, Mondorf, Luxembourg City has a casino and the latter's concerts and theatre are first rate. In the past few years, the country's image has changed from a nation of accordian players to a more classical aspect. These days, in summer, artistes such as Ray Charles will perform in the capital and recitals of *Carmen* or Verdi can be heard in Wiltz and Echternach.

To be frank, Luxembourgers, themselves, like to eat and drink for their evening's entertainment, socializing with their own friends or friendly foreigners in some pub or cafe, so there are plenty of roadside bistros.

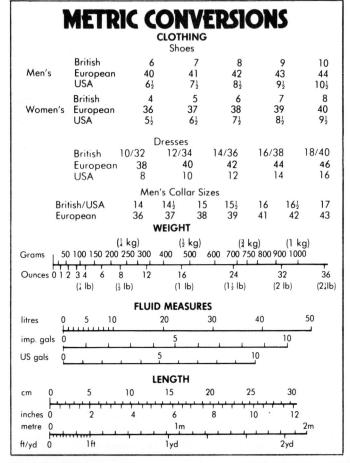

METRIC CONVERSIONS

CLOTHING
Shoes

	British	6	7	8	9	10
Men's	European	40	41	42	43	44
	USA	6½	7½	8½	9½	10½
	British	4	5	6	7	8
Women's	European	36	37	38	39	40
	USA	5½	6½	7½	8½	9½

Dresses

British	10/32	12/34	14/36	16/38	18/40
European	38	40	42	44	46
USA	8	10	12	14	16

Men's Collar Sizes

British/USA	14	14½	15	15½	16	16½	17
European	36	37	38	39	41	42	43

WEIGHT

	(¼ kg)	(½ kg)	(¾ kg)	(1 kg)
Grams	50 100 150 200 250 300	400 500	600 700 750 800 900 1000	
Ounces	0 1 2 3 4 6 8	12	16	24	32	36
	(¼ lb)	(½ lb)	(1 lb)	(1½ lb)	(2 lb)	(2¼ lb)

FLUID MEASURES

litres	0 5 10	20	30	40	50
imp. gals	0	5	10		
US gals	0	5	10		

LENGTH

cm	0	5	10	15	20	25	30
inches	0	2	4	6	8	10	12
metre	0		1m				2m
ft/yd	0	1ft	1yd		2yd		

WHAT YOU NEED TO KNOW

Chemist/pharmacy Most chemists are open Mon.–Fri. 0800/0900 to 1730/1800. For night time or weekend emergency prescriptions or medicines, ask the hotel concierge which is the nearest chemist open as they stay open in turns, changing weekly.

Churches Churches of different denominations will be found in all three countries, although there is a predominance of Roman Catholic ones in Belgium and Luxembourg. Services are held at fixed times but vary from place to place. You can obtain a list either from your hotel or the local tourist office, and times will be posted outside of each church.

Cigarettes and Tobacco Imported brands are available at most tobacconists but they cost more. Popular local brands include *Belga* (strong) and *Carlton* in Belgium; *Roxy* and *Lexington* in Holland; *Maryland* and *Ducal* in Luxembourg.

Electricity The voltage throughout is 220, 50 cycles.

Health Britain, as a member of the EEC has an agreement that medical advice and treatment will be provided on the same basis as for Benelux subjects. British visitors must have a certificate indicating that they are entitled to medical benefits under the British National Health Service. The certificate form E111, is issued by the local offices of the Department of Health and Social Security, which will first require the application form CM1. This form is part of the explanatory leaflet SA28. This gives full details of the health services in all EEC countries.

American visitors should ensure that their own medical insurance is extended to cover them while abroad. Insurance brokers or travel agents will advise and arrange the additional cover.

Doctors are listed in the 'Yellow Pages' under 'D' or 'M' (*medecins*) as are dentists. Hotels and chemists will also refer you. Do take out additional insurance before you depart for Benelux (see Insurance, p. 12).

Newspapers and Magazines The large hotels sell foreign journals as do some bookshops and kiosks in the major cities.

Photography No one minds being photographed although some museums and art galleries may not allow you to take your camera inside. Films are readily available at chemists and newsagents.

Police Belgium doesn't have traffic wardens and their police have given up wearing their white hats. Nowadays their uniform and caps are dark blue with the town badge on the shoulder. In Luxembourg, the municipal police wear black uniforms and caps in winter, beige in summer. National police (*gendarmes*) wear dark blue. The Dutch police also wear dark blue uniforms with a dark blue cap.

Postal Services Post offices are plentiful. In Belgium they are open in the main from 0900 to 1200 and again from 1400 to 1600 Mon.–Fri., except for those located near the railway station in larger towns, which remain open continuously from 0900 to 1700. Most post boxes are the wall hanging variety, painted red. Stamps may often be purchased at news kiosks and at hotels. In Holland, post offices are open 0900 to 1700 Mon.–Fri. Here, too, letter boxes are painted red and stamps are sold in tobacconists and card shops. Luxembourg City's post office near the station is open 24 hours; elsewhere only open 0900–1700 Mon.–Fri. and sometimes only half days. Post boxes are yellow and stamps are usually sold at souvenir shops.

Public Holidays Holland: New Year's Day, Good Friday (some shops open), Easter Monday, Queen's Birthday (April 30 – many shops open at least during the morning), Ascension Day, Whit Sunday and Monday, Christmas and Boxing Day. **Belgium:** All shops and public institutions are closed on the following days: New Year's Day, Easter Monday, Labour Day (May 1), Ascension Day, Whit Monday, Belgian National Day (July 21), Feast of the Assumption (August 15), All Saints (November 1), Armistice Day (November 11), Christmas Day. **Luxembourg:** New Year's Day, Easter Monday, May Day (May 1), Ascension Day, Whit Monday, National Day (June 23), Assumption Day (August 15), All Saints Day (November 1), Christmas Day, Boxing Day.

Rabies Rabid wild animals, principally foxes, are at large. Caution is essential when approaching any wild animals, or dogs roaming free from control. There is at present no effective preventive vaccine against rabies. A bite or scratch incurred through contact with a wild or stray animal should be washed immediately with soap and water, and medical advice sought.

The UK totally prohibits the importation of animals (including domestic pets) except under licence. One of the conditions of the licence is that the animals are retained in approved quarantine premises for up to six months. No exemptions are made for animals that have been vaccinated against rabies. Penalties for smuggling involve imprisonment, unlimited fines and the destruction of the animal.

Any animal being imported into the US must have a valid certificate of vaccination against rabies.

For details apply to the Ministry of Agriculture (Animal Health Division), Hook Rise South, Tolworth, Surbiton, Surrey KT6 7NF.

Shops Opening hours are usually: **Holland:** Most shops are open 0830/0900 to 1730/1800 Mon.–Fri. On Saturday food stores are generally open 0830/0900 to 1600, other shops until 1700. Some shops close lunchtime; some close later in the evening. All close one morning, one afternoon or one day a week, often Monday morning or Wednesday afternoon. In the resorts shops are often open in the evening and on weekends in season. **Belgium:** Most department stores are open 0900 to 1800. Some shut for lunch, from noon to 1400 in which case they stay open until 2000. Friday is generally a late night shopping day in most towns, when shops don't close until 2000–2100. **Luxembourg:** Most shops are open six days a week from 0800/0900 until 1800, but close for lunch normally 1200 to 1400. Most stores in Luxembourg City are closed Monday mornings.

Souvenirs Belgian craftsmen have long been famous for their skills, like those in Dinant who have been noted for their metal work since the Middle Ages. This is the place to buy handbeaten copper items. Liège is the home of Val-Saint-Lambert crystal and is well known for its sporting guns. Pewter ware is a good buy, it's made in Huy and has been for centuries. Spa's artists carve wooden wares. The handmade lace in Bruges and Brussels is exquisite if pricey and Belgian pralines and chocolates find their way all over the world. These and other souvenir buys are available in shops in many towns, at fixed prices. If you prefer the fun of haggling, try one of the markets, such as the Grand Sablon in Brussels or the Vogelmarkt in Antwerp.

They may not be wearing clogs in Holland any more, but they certainly sell miniature ones as souvenirs, in both wood and ceramic. The little Dutch dolls in national costume are an ideal gift for a child and a large selection of liqueurs is made in the Netherlands. Make sure you ascertain whether the Delft ware you see is genuine or not, unless you don't mind imitations – there are plenty of the latter on sale. It's Holland's best known ceramic ware although some pretty, traditional pottery is made in Makkum and Workum. Don't expect a bargain on Amsterdam's diamonds, but Leerdam's crystal may be cheaper than at home. Schoonhoven is known for its silverware and don't forget to bring home a cheese or two. All prices are fixed although haggling is acceptable in Dutch markets such as Amsterdam's flea market.

There's not a lot to buy in Luxembourg except for the wines which are excellent purchases. (If you don't drink them before you get home!) Luxembourg, is, however the home of Villeroy & Boch, the porcelain manufacturers. Their decorative plates depicting Grand Duchy landscapes are favourite souvenirs, as are the cast-iron miniature fire-backs known as *tåk* which often represent castles.

Telephone/Telegrams Holland: There is direct-dialling within Holland and from various places it is possible to direct-dial abroad, including from some call boxes. A local call costs Dfl 0.25 or Dfl 0.30 for unlimited duration. The operator's number and the emergency number varies from place to place but is always shown on public telephones. All calls may be made from post offices. **Belgium:** There is direct/dialling throughout including international calls, using BF 5 coins, which in tourist centres may be made from public call boxes. The cost of the latter, of course, will vary with distance and duration. A local three minute call from a telephone box requires a BF 10 or 20 coin and the operator is obtained by dialling 998. Emergency services are reached by dialling 900; police, 901. Telephone and telegraph offices may generally be found in or near train stations in major cities and are open 24 hours. **Luxembourg:** Direct-dialling may be done locally and in some cases internationally from call boxes. Cost of a local call is one five franc coin for three minutes except the capital where you can talk for as long as you like. It is best to make international calls from a post office. The operator is obtained by dialling 0010; emergency services, 012.

Time One hour ahead of GMT in winter; two hours ahead of GMT in summer. (As far as the UK is concerned, this means that the time is one hour ahead throughout the year.)

Tipping In restaurants which don't feature *all-inclusive* menus, it is customary to leave 15 per cent of the bill for the waiter (16 per cent in Belgium). When a service charge is already added, only leave small change if you wish. In Belgium, a porter or usherette gets 10 frs; lavatory attendants 5 frs; taxis include tips. In Luxembourg, the first piece of luggage costs a fixed 20 fr rate and each additional piece, 15 frs. Usherettes aren't tipped; toilet attendants, 5 frs and ten per cent to taxis.

Toilets Public toilets may be found in cities and resorts throughout the Benelux countries. They are particularly clean in Holland including those at the filling stations which may be used free.

CUSTOMS

Members of EEC countries entering any of the Benelux countries are allowed to import a greater quantity of cigarettes, spirits, wines and perfume than residents of other countries (eg. Canada and USA). UK residents may import duty free up to 300 cigarettes or 150 cigarillos or 75 cigars or 400gm tobacco. Additionally, they may bring in up to 1.5 litres of spirits more than 22 per cent proof or up to 3 litres, less than 22 per cent proof (eg. fortified wines). Plus up to 3 litres of still wines. (If you are travelling from Luxembourg to Belgium, you may bring up to 8 litres of still wine across the border.) You're allowed up to 75gm of perfume and ⅜ths of a litre of toilet water.

Articles for personal use or meant as small gifts for residents of Benelux are not dutiable. These may include personal jewellery, two cameras plus a reasonable amount of film, two cine cameras, tape recorder, binoculars, portable typewriter, most reasonable tenting, camping and sports equipment.

USEFUL ADDRESSES

Netherlands National Tourist Offices, 143 New Bond St., London W.1. (01 499 9367); Bezuidenhoutseweg 2, NL-2594 AV, The Hague (70 814191); One Dundas St. West, Box 19, Suite 2108, Toronto, Ontario M5G 1Z3 (416.598 2830); 576 Fifth Ave., New York 10036 (212 245 5320).
Belgian National Tourist Offices 38 Dover St., London, W.1. (01 499 5379); Grasmarkt 61, Rue du Marché aux Herbes, 1000 Brussels (02 513 90 90); Avenue de la Gare 51; 745 Fifth Ave., New York 10022 (212 758 8130).
Luxembourg National Tourist Offices 36/37 Piccadilly, London W.1. (01 434 2800); Avenue de la Gare 51, Luxembourg City (352 48 79 99); 801 2nd Ave., New York, 10017 (212 370 9850).
Provincial VVV: VVV Groningen: Grote Markt 23, 9712 HR Groningen, (139700); VVV Friesland: Stationsplein 1, 8911 AC Leeuwarden, (32224); VVV Drenthe: Postbus 95, 9400 AB Assen, (14324); VVV

Duty-free allowances *subject to change*		Goods bought in a duty-free shop	Goods bought in EEC
Tobacco	Cigarettes or	200	300
Double if you live outside Europe	Cigars *small* or	100	150
	Cigars *large* or	50	75
	Pipe tobacco	250 gm	400 gm
Alcohol	Spirits *over 38.8° proof* or Fortified or sparkling wine plus	1 litre	1½ litres
		2 litres	3 litres
	Table wine	2 litres	4 litres
Perfume		50 gm	75 gm
Toilet water		250 cc	375 cc
Other goods		£28	£120

US customs permit duty-free $300 retail value of purchases per person, 1 quart of liquor per person over 21, and 100 cigars per person.

Overijssel: De Werf 1, 7607 HH Almelo, (10266); Gelderland: Postbus 988, 6800 AZ Arnhem, (185 513713); VVV Utrecht: Vredenburg 90, 3511 BD Utrecht, (30 314132); VVV Noord-Holland: Postbus 3901, 1001 AS Amsterdam (20 266444); VVV Zuid-Holland: Markt 85, 2611 GS Delft, (15 126100); VVV Zeeland: Postbus 123, 4330 AC Middelburg, (28051); VVV Noord-Brabant: Postbus 3399, 4800 DJ Breda, (76 225733); VVV Limburg: Postbus 811, 6300 AV Valkenburg, (13993); VVV Amsterdam: Postbus 3901, 1001 AS Amsterdam (20 266444); VVV Rotterdam: Stadhuisplein 19, 3012 AR Rotterdam, (10 136000); VVV Den Haag: Postbus 85973, 2508 CR Den Haag, (70 546200).

Belgian provincial offices Toeristische Federatie van de Provincie Antwerpen, 11 Karel Oomsstraat, 2000 Antwerpen, (031 62810); Toeristische Federatie van Brabant, Grasmarkt 61, Rue Marché aux Herbes, 1000 Brussels, (2 513 07 50); Fédération du Tourisme de la Province du Hainaut, Rue des Clercs 31, 7000 Mons, (65 31 61 01); Provinciaal Verbond voor Toerisme in Limburg, Domein Bokrijk, 3600 Genk, (11 22 29 58); Fédération du Tourisme de la Province de Liège, Boulevard de la Sauvenière 77, 4000 Liège, (41 32 5210); Fédération Touristique du Luxembourg Belge, Quai de L'Ourthe 9, 6980 La Roche-en-Ardenne, (84 41 10 11); Fédération du Tourisme de la Province de Namur, Rue Notre-Dame 3, 5000 Namur, (81 22 29 98); Federatie voor Toerisme in Oost-Vlaanderen, Koningin Maria-Hendrikaplein 64, 9000 Gent, (91 22 16 27); Westtoerism, Vlamingstraat 55, 8000 Brugge, (50 33 73 44); Dienst voor Toerism, Suikerrui 19, 2000 Antwerpen, (32 32 01 03).

Embassies Netherlands, 38 Hyde Park Gate, London SW7 (01 584 5040); 4200 Linnean Ave., NW, Washington, DC. 20008 (202 244 5500). **Belgium** 103 Eaton Sq., London SW1 (01 235 5422); 3330 Garfield St., NW Washington, DC, 20008 (202 333 6900). **Luxembourg** 27 Wilton Crescent, London SW1 (01 235 6961); 2200 Massachussetts Ave, NW, Washington, DC 20008 (202 265 4171).

Air Services British Airways, Heathrow Airport, Middlesex, (01 370 5411); British Caledonian Airways, Gatwick Airport, Horley, Surrey, (01 668 4222); KLM, New Bond St., London W1, (01 492 0336); Sabena World Airlines, 36 Piccadilly, London W1 (01 437 6950); British Midland Airways, 52 Curzon St., London W1 (01 492 0864); Air Anglia, Norwich Airport, Norwich, Norfolk (0603 44288); British Island Airways, Berkeley House, 51–53 High St., Redhill (0737 65921).

Sea Ferries Sealink, Car Ferry Centre, Eversholt House, Eversholt St., London NW1 (01 387 1234); Norfolk Line, Southgates Rd., Great Yarmouth, Norfolk (0493 56133); North Sea Ferries, King George Dock, Hedon Rd., Hull HU9 5QA, (0482 795141); Olau Line, Ferry Terminal Bldg., Sheerness, Kent ME12 1SN, (0795 666 666); Townsend Thorensen, Car Ferry Centre, Russell St., Dover, Kent CT16 1QB, (0304 223605); Hoverspeed, Hoverport, Western Docks, Dover, Kent, (0304 208013).

Rail Services British Railways Travel Centre, 4 Lower Regent St., London SW1, (01 930 4792); Belgian National Railroads, 22/25A Sackville St., London W1, (01 734 1491); Belgian National Railroads, 745 Fifth Ave., New York 10019, (212 758 8130); Netherlands Railways, 4 New Burlington St., London W1, (01 734 3301).

THE LANGUAGE

Dutch is a Germanic language spoken by the people of the Netherlands, and also by a good proportion of the Belgians. The Dutch appear to be natural linguists, speaking a variety of foreign languages including very good English – which is just as well as their national tongue is difficult to pronounce. (If you are Scottish, it will be easier.)

A type of Dutch – Flemish – is spoken in the northern provinces of Belgium, although the Netherlanders often claim they can't understand Flemish. You'll find it spoken in Antwerp, Limburg, East and West Flanders, where place names and menus are usually written in both Flemish and French. French is spoken by 3.6 million Walloons (36 per cent of the population) who live in the southern provinces of Brabant, Hainaut, Liège, Luxembourg and Namur. In the eastern part of the country, near the German border, there are about 65,000 German-speaking people.

Most Luxembourgers are tri-lingual. Their own language, Luxembourgeois, is the everyday language although French is the official one and everyone seems to speak German. In the past few years, knowledge of English has become more common.

KEY WORDS AND PHRASES

English	French	Dutch
Yes	Oui	Ja
No	Non	Nee
Please	S'il vous plaît	Als het U belieft
Thank you	Merci	Dank U
Good morning	Bonjour	Goede morgen
Good afternoon	Bonjour	Goede middag
Good evening	Bonsoir	Goedenavond
Goodnight	Bonne nuit	Goede nacht
Goodbye	Au revoir	Tot ziens
Where is . . .?	Où est . . .?	Waar is . . .?
. . . Street	la rue . . .	de . . . straat
. . . Square	la place . . .	de . . . plaats
the church	l'église	de kerk
the museum	le musée	het museum
the police station	le poste de police	het politie bureau
right	à droite	rechts
left	à gauche	links
straight on	tout droit	rechtuit
above	en haut	boven
below	en bas	beneden
When	Quand	Wanneer
When is . . . open?	A quelle heure . . . est ouvert(e)?	Wanneer is geopend . . .?
the town hall	l'hôtel de ville	het stadthuis
the post office	le bureau de poste	het postkantoor
the bank	la banque	de bank
the station	la gare	het station
the hotel	l'hôtel	het hotel
I want a room	Je voudrais une chambre	Ik wil graag een kamer
a single room	pour une personne	eenpersoonskamer
a double room	pour deux personnes	tweepersoonskamer
with a shower	avec douche	met douche
the key	la clef	de sleutel
a doctor	un medécin	de dokter
How much is . . .?	Combien coûte?	Hoeveel kost . . .?
breakfast	le petit dejeuner	het ontbijt
lunch	le dejeuner	het middagmaal
dinner	le diner	het avondmaal
much, many	beaucoup	veel
little, few	peu	weinig
the bill	l'addition	de rekening
to eat	manger	eten
to drink	boire	drinken
to pay	payer	betalen
I do not understand you.	Je ne comprends pas.	Ik versta U niet.
Do you speak English?	Parlez-vous Anglais?	Spreekt U Engels?
Will you help me?	Voulez-vous aider moi?	Wilt U mij helpen?

Traditional dress in Volendam

Keukenhof Gardens

Lifting bridge, Arnhem

The New Church (1383), Delft

Rokin, Amsterdam

NOORD-HOLLAND ZUID-HOLLAND UTRECHT

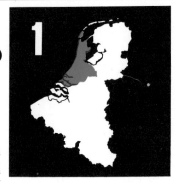

Industry mixes happily with history and agriculture in these three provinces. Noord-Holland and Zuid-Holland which receive the majority of the country's visitors, are mostly below sea level, but the coastal dunes keep the sea out. The soil behind the dunes provides the fertile basis for bulb growing – and this is the region for flowers. The culture is worth many thousands of guilders annually in export value with tulips one of the prime flowers grown. Research and auctions take place in Lisse in the area of the world-renowned Keukenhof Gardens. Flowering commences at the end of March and lasts until mid-May.

Even in the most commercial centres, such as the great city/port of Rotterdam, there is plenty to interest the tourist besides the large shipyards. Along the Rivers Waal, Maas (Meuse) and Lek, there is industry, but the landscape of lakes, canals and dykes has not been spoiled. In these provinces there are tiny villages whose local inhabitants wear colourful national costume and the largest conglomeration of working windmills. This is the region for Gothic churches, baroque town halls and gracious almshouses. This is the region for the great cities of Amsterdam and The Hague – living museums of 17th-century architecture. Many famous people, like Vermeer and Rembrandt, were born in this part of the Netherlands, along with revolutionary thinkers like Erasmus and great physicists such as Van Leeuwenhoek.

And in Utrecht, Holland's tiniest province, streams weave a silver thread through the woods and the only towns of any size are Utrecht and Amersfoort.

Eels and apples Eel soup is a Zuid-Holland delicacy but in Aalsmeer, try *eelsyrup*. No mixture is too strange in Holland. A popular one is a combination of buttermilk, cherry juice, honey, sugar and cinnamon! Dutch fruit is always high quality – in season, Aalsmeer strawberries are a dessert treat all by themselves, but in Zuid-Holland, bacon is served with pears and in Utrecht, try *stichter applecakes*. When you

see *houtssnip* on the menu, it's a cheese sandwich using one slice of white bread and one of pumpernickel. Zuid-Holland's beers are world famous.

Festivals and events Mid-May: national open air flower show at Keukenhof and in Lisse. April 26: flower pageant in Lisse, and late May *Liliade*. May 24: flower pageant in Rotterdam. June–September: international rose show at The Hague with a rose festival in July. May 31: international balloon race in Scheveningen. Mid-April–mid-September: Alkmaar cheese markets on Fridays. June–August: folklore events in Hoorn and June/July in Medemblik. Mid-August: international *Nevo* folk dance festival in Leiden. The Holland Festival during the summer months with plays, concerts, ballet, etc. in Amsterdam, Rotterdam, Utrecht and The Hague. Pre-Christmas candlelight tours of Gouda.

Aalsmeer   K8

(pop. 20,900). Venue of the world's biggest **flower auction**, situated on the Westeinder lakes in Noord-Holland. Europe's most important flower auction hall, St Trowle Aalsmeerse Bloemenveiling, may be visited every morning Mon.–Fri. until 1100. The buyers themselves, come early and bid by pressing electric buttons – the bidding continues until all the flowers have been sold which is around 1130 so try to get here early. Look out for the blooms arriving – they reach the auction hall on long flat floating punts.

Numerous auctions are held in this region as there are countless nurseries. In town you can visit a workshop overlooking the Zijdstraat which makes wooden shoes, and see the 100-year-old windmill. Sport facilities include sailing and rowing on the surrounding lakes.

The *Bloemencorso* (flower festival) is held in Aalsmeer on the first Saturday of September when over two million flowers are used to decorate huge floats. *Amsterdam 19km/12mi.*

Cheese market, Alkmaar

Alkmaar   G8

(pop. 69,000) A pretty little olde worlde town just north of Haarlem in Noord-Holland, where victory was first assured in the Eighty Years War against Spain. It became a city in 1254, but with a network of canals lined by gabled houses, it has retained an old atmosphere. See the Gothic **Church of St Laurens** (1470–1516) which houses the Netherlands' oldest pipe organ, built by Jacob Van Campen. Also the **City Museum** in the early 16th-century Town Hall on Langestraat, which has 17th-century paintings.

Alkmaar is most famous, though, for its **cheese market** held between April and September on Friday mornings, 1000–1200 in front of the **Waag** Weigh House. At this time, white-costumed guild porters wearing coloured hats, carry wooden cradles filled with large round cheeses as they do a fast jog to the Weigh House (converted from a 15th-century chapel). Its carillon tinkles out folk tunes while the market is in progress. Tourists are recommended to be at the market place by 0930 to have the best view. In summer the Dutch railways run special 'cheese trains'. *Amsterdam 41km/25mi.*

Alphen aan den Rijn   M7

(pop. 53,000) A small, busy industrial town noted mostly for its interesting bird park, the **Avifauna Bird Sanctuary**, open Mar.–Oct. from 0900 and Sundays from 1300. Thousands of birds of hundreds of species are housed here. Tropical birds live amidst exotic plants in heated glass houses, while polar birds splash about in their own houses which resemble icy caves. Ostriches and emus stroll the lawns and at night the whole place is floodlit. Boat trips to Avifauna can be made daily from The Hague, Rotterdam and Amsterdam and there are also organized boat trips from Alphen in summer on the Brasemermeer Lake. **Alphen**, 3km/2mi to the east, is a district specializing in flowering plants and shrubs. Small trees are trimmed into a variety of shapes. *Amsterdam 36km/22.5mi.*

Amersfoort   M13

(pop. 88,000) The second largest city in the province of Utrecht and a most atmospheric one. It was granted its first charter in 1259 and is still surrounded by a double ring of canals. Entire houses are built on and into the immense city walls behind which canals flow along quiet back streets. The city centre, with its old streets and stocks, is straight from the Middle Ages.

See the four handsome city gates, particularly the 15th-century **Koppelpoort** over the River Eem. The 13th-century **Kamperbinnenpoort** and the 15th-century **Waterpoort Monnickendam** also show evidence that this was formerly a fortress town. The **Onze Lieve Vrouwe Church** has a 15th-century carillon tower and a unique bell-ringing school. Most of the bell melodies heard from towers in other cities are produced by its pupils. **St Peters Blocklandsgasthuis**, a 16th-century almshouse, has furniture and eating utensils of the period and the **Flehite Museum** on Westsingel has interesting antiquities from Amersfoort's past. Jacob van Campen (who designed the Royal Palace in Antwerp among other things) is buried in **St Joris Church** which has some beautiful frescoes. There is a

The Koppelpoort, Amersfoort

flower market on the Havik and Zonnehot Hall is a regular exhibition for Dutch and foreign art. *Amsterdam 51km/32mi.*

Amsterdam   J9

(pop. 719,000) Capital of the Netherlands, Amsterdam has 4000 old merchants' houses and warehouses and more than 1000 bridges spanning the famous canals encircling the heart of the old city. It was originally a fishing community where the Rivers Amstel and IJ met. The first dam built across the Amstel is now the capital's central square, Dam Square, and was the major key to Amsterdam's development. The city became such an important trading centre that it was granted toll and tax exemption.

The first canal was a moat, but as the city expanded, a second, third and fourth ring of canals were built so that finally the Indies cargoes could be unloaded in the centre of Amsterdam directly from the ships which had brought them. Because of its commercial activities, the city enjoyed a Golden Age in the 17th century. Merchants' houses with their 'gingerbread' appearance lining important canals like the Herengracht and Singel are one of the city's biggest attractions. These houses were deliberately built tall and narrow because in the past, tax was calculated according to the size of a building's frontage.

What to See With four concentric canals and three major squares, Amsterdam is best explored on foot. Do, however, take one of the glass-topped boat tours through the canals. There are several departure docks which are marked by the sign *Rondvaart* (round trip). Boats leave at about half hour intervals – in summer, often every fifteen minutes. Major departure point is opposite Centraal station and the trips last a little over an hour.

Culturally, Amsterdam excels – there are more than 40 museums. One of the main ones is **Rijksmuseum**, 42 Stadhouderskade, which needs a minimum of two hours for a browse through. It contains the biggest art and applied arts and crafts collection in the Netherlands, with primary emphasis on such 17th-century masters as Rembrandt. (Open Tues.–Sat. 1000–1700; Sundays, 1300–1700). Another important museum is the **Van Gogh**, Paulus Potterstraat, which contains the most complete collection of Van Gogh's paintings, original letters, drawings, etc. to be found anywhere. (Open Tues.–Sat., 1000–1700; Sun., 1300–1700). In addition to the host of other museums, see **Anne Frank's house** at 263 Prinsengracht, open Mon.–Sat., 0900–1700; Sun., 1000–1700.

Although Amsterdam has few palaces, it has a legion of churches. There are small

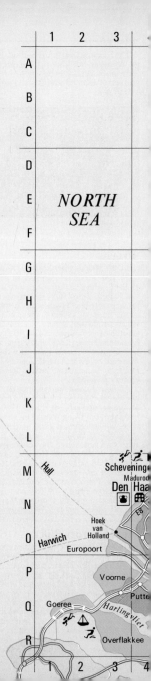

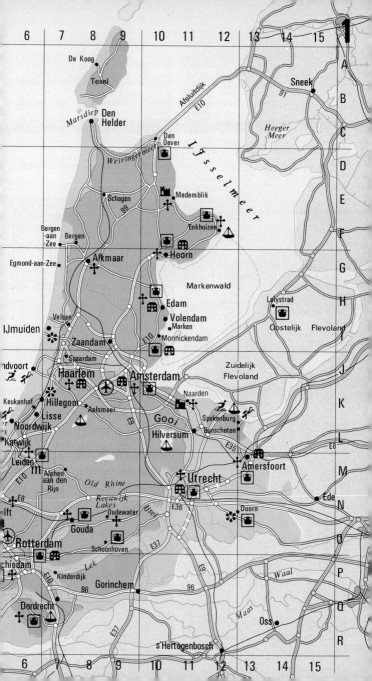

ones like the **Beguine Court** and old ones like the elaborate **Oude Kerk**. The **Westerkerk** is a typical Dutch Protestant church, open Tues. and Thurs. from 1400–1600.

Among the tour possibilities, take the one to **Heineken's Brewery**, 78 Stadhouderskade, one of the two breweries offering free visit and sampling, Mon.–Fri., 1000–1130. Visit one of the diamond factories such as A. Van Moppes and Zoon, 2 Albert Cuypstraat where you can see all phases of diamond cutting, shaping and polishing. The world's smallest diamond is displayed here along with replicas of the most famous ones like the Hope Diamond. Visits may be made from 0900–1700.

One of the best streets for shopping is Kalverstraat but there's a flea market in Valkenburgerstraat and a flower market in the city centre.

Where to Stay There's a full range of hotels in all styles to be found in the city centre. The Sonesta, for example is three minutes from Dam Square and other familiar chain names include Hilton, Grand Met and Howard Johnson, plus the Okura Inter-

On the Keizersgracht

Street organ

Market in Albert Cuypstraat

Sightseeing waterbus

continental. There are lower priced hotels, boarding houses and a youth hostel besides.

Eating Out A rich choice of cafes and restaurants includes those which offer a reasonable, fixed price 'tourist menu'. One of the most interesting eating places, although somewhat expensive, is 'Five Flies' in a 'Golden Age' setting on Spuistraat.

Entertainment There's a wide range of nightlife from that in the 'Red Light' district (Nieuwendijk-Zeedijk) to the host of nightclubs and discotheques around Rembrandtsplein, Thorbeckeplein and Leidseplein. Among the top clubs is the *Piccadilly* on Thorbeckeplein, recommended for its floor show. An ever-popular disco is *King's Club* on Korte Leidsedwarsstraat. If you fancy gin sampling in one of the old taverns, try Wijnand Fockink or Bols Taverne.

Amsterdam's 47 cinemas show films in their original language and theatres are plentiful. The Concertgebouw is the home of the orchestra of the same name and Amsterdam's Philharmonic Orchestra. Every June the *Holland Festival* includes

Three-part tram

On the Herengracht

The Rijksmuseum

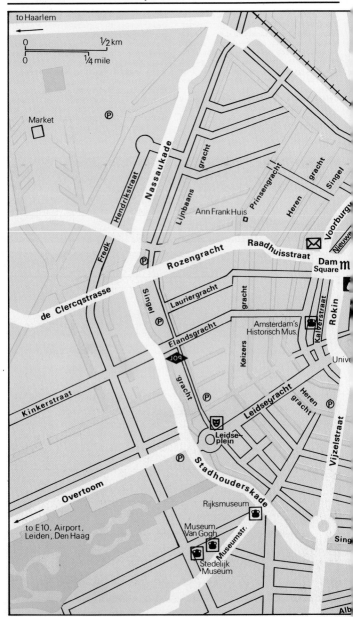

to Haarlem

0 _____ ½ km
0 _____ ¼ mile

Market

Hendrikstraat

Nassaukade

Lijnbaans gracht

Ann Frank Huis

Prinsengracht

Heren gracht

gracht

Singel

Voorburgw

Fredk.

de Clercqstrasse

Rozengracht

Raadhuisstraat

Nieuwe

Dam Square

Singel

Lauriergracht

Elandsgracht

gracht

Keizers

Amsterdam's Historisch Mus.

Kalverstraat

Rokin

Unive

gracht

Kinkerstraat

Leidsegracht

Heren gracht

Vijzelstraat

Leidse-plein

Stadhouderskade

Overtoom

to E10, Airport, Leiden, Den Haag

Rijksmuseum

Museum Van Gogh

Museumstr.

Stedelijk Museum

Sing

Alb

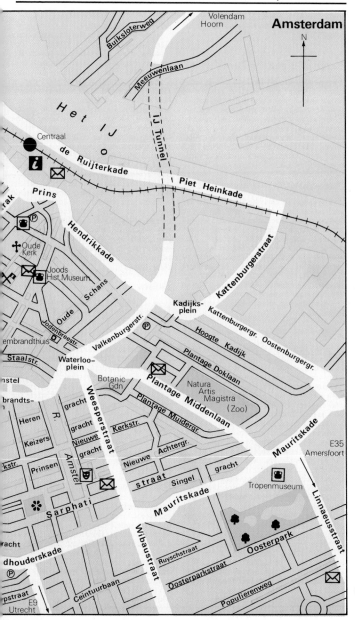

Amsterdam

N

Volendam
Hoorn

Buiksloterweg

Meeuwenlaan

IJ Tunnel

H e t   I J

Centraal

de Ruijterkade

Piet Heinkade

Prins

Hendrikkade

Kattenburgerstraat

Oude Kerk

Joods Hist. Museum

Schans

Kadijks-plein

Kattenburgergr. Oostenburgergr.

Oude

Jodenbreestr.

embrandthuis

Valkenburgerstr.

Hoogte Kadijk

Staalstr.

Waterloo-plein

Plantage Doklaan

Plantage Middenlaan

nstel

Botanic Gdn

Plantage Muidergr.

Natura Artis Magistra (Zoo)

brandts-

gracht

Weesperstraat

Kerkstr.

Heren

gracht

Nieuwe Achtergr.

Mauritskade

E35
Amersfoort

Keizers

Nieuwe

straat

Singel

gracht

kstr.

Prinsen

Amstel

Tropenmuseum

Linnaeusstraat

Sarphati

Mauritskade

racht

Oosterpark

dhouderskade

Ruyschstraat

pstraat

Wibaustraat

Oosterparkstraat

E9
Utrecht

Ceintuurbaan

Populierenweg

major concerts, operas, dance, theatre and film. *Rotterdam 76km/47.5mi, The Hague 60km/37.5m.*

Bergen/Bergen aan Zee   F7

Two popular Noord-Holland resorts separated by dunes and forest. A number of artists live in the village of Bergen and in summer exhibit their art in the open air. There's also a partly ruined 14th-century church here. Bergen aan Zee is a seaside resort 5km/3mi away where there is a good dune-backed beach, woods, moors and some tiny lakes. Sports include tennis, mini-golf, riding and fishing.

Bunschoten/Spakenburg   L12

Two villages of the IJsselmeer noted for their colourful costumes. The distinctive feature of the girls' costume is the *kraplap* made of brightly flowered cotton, heavily starched and worn with lace caps. And nobody minds being photographed in it. Fishing has virtually finished here to be replaced by an emphasis on pleasure watersports. In the heart of Spakenburg, however, an unusual old shipyard is still in use, and several establishments in the vicinity continue to smoke eels. *Amsterdam 46km/29mi.*

Delft   N5

(pop. 86,000) This is the typical picture-postcard town that reminds the tourist of all Holland. Located a short way from Rotterdam, on the main highway to The Hague and Amsterdam, Delft is a pretty little town with lots of canals lined with stately trees and crossed by white bridges. The elaborate gabled houses complete the image. Although water taxis run here in summer, it is more rewarding to explore Delft on foot.

One of its most charming canals is the Voldersgracht and one of the most stately is the Koornmarkt, spanned by high arching bridges. The city's oldest waterway is the **Oude Delft Canal** dating back to 1000. Close by is the oldest dwelling, the **Gemeenlandshuis**, used by the Counts of Holland during their visits.

See the **Nieuwe Kerk** in the Grote Markt, a well designed church with a tall spire and some lovely stained glass. Founder of the Netherlands, William of Orange ('The Silent') is buried here along with other members of Holland's royalty. William The Silent lived, and was murdered in 1584, in the 15th-century **Prinsenhof**, located opposite the **Oude Kerk** (13th-century). You can still see the assassin's bullet holes at the bottom of the winding staircase. Graves of several famous admirals are in the Oude Kerk.

In the **Town Hall** on the Grote Markt is a collection of paintings by Delft artists. The building itself is designed in Italian Renaissance style, rebuilt after a 1618 fire. (Open 1000–1700 daily; Sun. 1300–1700). The market square is the liveliest part of Delft – an annual floodlit tattoo takes place here at the end of August. The Prinsenhof holds an annual art and antiques fair around Oct./Nov. Beyond that building is the **Lambert van Meerten Museum** which contains an excellent collection of fine old Delft tiles and early Delft pottery. Another unusual little museum is the **Paul Téter van Elven Museum** at the 67 Koornmarkt, once a 16th-century artist's house.

Although many copies of Delft's famous blue and white patterned china are made and sold, you can watch the authentic hand made variety being produced at **De Porceleyne Fles** and **De Delftse Pauw**, two major factories, whose names mean 'The Porcelain Bottle' and 'The Delft Peacock', which have been making that celebrated porcelain since the 17th century. *Rotterdam 16km/10mi.*

Doorn   N13

(pop. 11,000) In the province of Utrecht, Doorn was the home from 1920 to 1941 of exiled Emperor Wilhelm II, Kaiser of Germany. The manor house where he lived is now a museum containing a vast collection of memorabilia connected with the former German Royal House, not to mention such treasures as Frederick the Great's snuff boxes, Gobelin tapestries, magnificent furniture and silver. The Kaiser's remains are in an adjoining mausoleum while the park has conifers imported from all over the world.

Huis Doorn is open to the public from Mar.–Oct., Mon.–Sat. 0900–1230 and 1300–1700; Sun. 1300–1700. *Utrecht 21km/13mi.*

Dordrecht   Q7

(pop. 106,000) The oldest city in the province of Zuid-Holland. Its location, between the Rhine and Meuse, made it one of the Netherlands' most important towns as this river junction is said to be one of the world's busiest. Dordrecht was founded c.1008, became a leading centre in 1220 and was fortified in 1271. It was one of the first Protestant cities to join the 'Sea Beggars', a band of loosely united pirates who supported William of Orange in his struggle to rid the Netherlands of the Spanish in the 17th century.

Several painters were born in Dordrecht

including Bols, Cuyp, Maes and Van Hoogstraten. A good selection of their paintings are housed in the **Dordrecht Museum** in Museumstraat, open Tues.–Sat. 1000–1700; Sun. and Mon. 1300–1700. The city was also the home of the De Witt brothers, prominent 17th-century politicians. Local antiques, such as model ships, antique toys and period furnishings can be seen in the **Van Gijn Museum**. (Open daily 1000–1700 except Mon.)

See also the **Grote Kerk** (1064) which was enlarged during the 12th and 13th centuries, rebuilt in 1457 after the fire that destroyed Dordrecht, which accounts for its Gothic arches. It has a particularly fine interior including a 3600-pipe organ dating from 1672; a white marble pulpit (1756) which has a carved mahogany canopy weighing more than a ton and standing 9m/30ft high. Carved choir stalls show the world's history; stained glass windows depict Dordrecht's own history. From the church, cross the canal to Voorstraat and turn left to the Groenmarkt, to find (Number 31) a beautiful old house. Or walk along the Wijnstraat which is lined by lovely old gabled houses. At the end of it, you will reach the 17th-century **Groothoofdspoort** gate, meeting point of the Rivers Merwede, Noord and Oudemass.

This riverside area is Dordrecht's most picturesque. Today the town is a major ship-building and yachting centre and in summer many visitors take advantage of the river for water activities such as boating and swimming. *Rotterdam 24km/15mi.*

Edam   H10

(pop. 22,000) A town in Noord-Holland most famous for its round, red-skinned cheeses made from lightly skimmed milk with a 40 per cent fat content. In the cheese weighing house on the Kaasmarkt, there is an interesting collection of cheese-making utensils.

Most of the historical sites are on the Damplein, including the **Town Hall** (1737) decorated with fine stucco work and with a magnificent 18th-century council room inside. The **Municipal Museum** is in a 17th-century sea captain's house and contains some odd paintings by a few of Edam's more eccentric former citizens. Its floating cellar is unusual – rising and falling with the swell of the water beneath it. The **Grote Kerk** (15th-century) of St Nicolas has some valuable stained glass from the 16th century; rare books; and a 17th-century classroom with its original desks. The biggest landmark is the **Speeltoren** with its old carillon cast in Malines. *Amsterdam 22km/14mi.*

Egmond aan Zee   G7

(pop. 4500) A popular Noord-Holland resort with a large sandy beach that provides safe bathing for all the family. It's a lively place with dancing, tennis, a children's playground and other amusements. In **Egmond aan de Hoef** (part of the resort), there is a 15th-century church and some castle remains. In another part, **Egmond Binnen**, there is the Abbey of Egmond, founded in 740 by St Adalbert, a Northumbrian missionary. The modern part of town lies between these two old parts. Surrounding dunes are ideal for walking and you could walk to Alkmaar from here in an hour and a half. *Amsterdam 41km/26mi.*

Enkhuizen   F12

(pop. 14,000) Once a bustling Zuider Zee harbour, though there aren't as many people living here now as there were in the 17th century and its large herring fleet no longer exists. There is still plenty here to interest tourists. The imposing, double-towered **Drommedaris** (1540) by the harbour front is a gateway whose beautiful carillon ranks with that of Edam. The main street is Westerstraat, lined with old houses such as the **Herenhuis**. It runs from the 17th-century **Westerpoort** gate. Also see: the **Westerkerk** which has handsome wood vaulting, a fine 16th-century rood screen, organ, manuscripts and tapestries. Opposite is the old mint and further along there is a 17th-century orphanage. The **Zuiderkerk** (15th-century) has a 43-bell carillon and painted vaults.

The museum in the former weigh bridge (16th-century) in the Kaasmarkt displays a collection of 17th-century medical equipment. (Open weekdays 1000–1700.) Another museum is housed in the 17th-century **Town Hall** in Breetstraat with Gobelin tapestries, paintings by Paulus Potter and a coin collection. Some say that the best museum is the open-air **Zuider Zee Museum** which opened in 1983, after eighteen years in the building, to show as many elements as possible of Zuider Zee culture.

(In 1932 the Zuider Zee was sealed off from the North Sea by the Afsluitdijk dam, turned into a fresh-water lake and renamed 'IJsselmeer'.)

One part of the museum is its 130 houses along streets, canals and alleys, providing a picture of life between 1880–1932. The other part or **Binnenmuseum** has a ship hall housing old sailing ships, traditional costumes and interiors, plus a collection of model ships. The former is open daily Apr.–Oct., 1000–1700; the latter Feb.–Dec., Mon.–Sat., 1000–1700, Sun., 1200–1700.

In summer, there are ferry services from Enkhuizen to **Staveren** and the former island of **Urk**. *Amsterdam 62km/39mi.*

Gouda   O7

(pop. 59,000) The Zuid-Holland town most famous for its yellow cheese. During the summer season, on Thursdays from 0900–

Dutch cheeses

1200, there is a cheese market in front of the **Waag** (weigh house). Instead of the porters used at Alkmaar, painted farm wagons are used to carry the cheese and you can sample some in the weigh house itself. Gouda is also known for the manufacture of clay pipes. You can see them in the **De Mooriaan Museum** in Westhave (one of Gouda's most picturesque streets) and also in the **Goedewaagen** factory.

The Municipal Museum is housed in the former St Catherine's Hospice (**Catharina Gasthuis**), Oosthaven 10. Here you can see a collection of torture instruments, paintings including some by Rubens, 17th-, 18th- and 19th-century furnished rooms and some unique *objets d'art* like Countess Jacqueline of Bavaria's golden chalice (1465) said to be the finest in existence. (Open weekdays, 1000–1700; Sun. 1400–1700.)

The stained-glass windows in the **Janskerk** are also said to be the finest in the Netherlands. The church (built in the 15th century and rebuilt in the 16th century after a fire) has the largest nave in the country and contains 64 stained-glass windows, 14 filled with 16th-century Burgundian glass and some 12 of which are accredited to Wouter and Dirk Crabeth. They portray figures of the time like William of Orange, Philip II of Spain and Mary Tudor.

In summer, boat and bus trips leave for day excursions to the **Reeuwijk Lakes**. *Rotterdam 23km/14mi.*

Haarlem   J7

(pop. 160,000) A typical Dutch residential town. Founded in the 10th century, it received its Charter in 1245, was besieged by the Spaniards from late 1572–mid-1573 when the city surrendered, and its citizens massacred.

You'll find the centre of the city well preserved with a number of interesting buildings bordering its main historic square. The **Church of St Bavo** (15th- to 16th-century) has a beautiful interior with a cross-vaulted cedar roof supported by 28 columns. Ball shot from a siege cannon in 1573 still lies embedded in its walls and its marvellous organ has been played by Mozart. The church also houses the tomb of Frans Hals. The Dutch Renaissance **Vleeshal** (meat market) is renowned for its fancy gabling and its coloured shutters. There's an 18th-century **Vishal** (fish hall) and a 13th-century **Town Hall** with a candle-lit and tapestried council chamber, open 0900–1230 and 1500–1700, Mon.–Fri., Sat. 0900–1200.

Haarlem has a number of photogenic gabled houses and almshouses. The **Frans Hals Museum** is one of them at Groot Heiligland 62. At night, the inner courtyard of the museum is flood-lit and the interior candle-lit, and from mid-June to mid-August, plus Easter and Whitsun weekends, musical recitals are given here on Saturday evenings. (Open normally Mon.–Sat. 1000–1700; Sun. 1300–1700.)

Among the city's interesting museums, visit the **Teijlers Museum** with its collection of old prints and surgical appliances; **Cruquies Museum** (a former steam pumping station) close to the Heemstede where land reclamation techniques are shown. **Visschoppelijk Museum** at Janenstraat 79 displays excellent ecclesiastical paintings, vestments and porcelain. (Open 1000–1700 daily, Sun. 1300–1600.)

As a reminder that Haarlem lies in the midst of bulb fields, in spring 20 Haarlem girls are chosen to greet tourists with a 'welcome flower'. At nearby **Hartenkamp**, 3km/2mi away, the Linnaeushof flower exhibition is held April–October. *Amsterdam 21km/13mi.*

The Hague (Den Haag)   N4

(pop. 470,000) The seat of Dutch government, situated by the North Sea, with three royal palaces, many parks, the Knights Hall, ministeries and diplomatic offices. The Dutch name means 'hedge' since the city grew up around the castle built by the Counts of Holland in the 13th century.

The original hunting lodge, **Binnenhof** is now greatly enlarged and houses the parliament. In the 16th century when it was no longer a stronghold, it was shuttled back and forth between the Spaniards and Dutch. Dutch 17th-century stadholders eventually turned it into one of Europe's most brilliant courts, it welcomed the exiled Charles II. The Binnenhof itself is reached through the 17th-century **Grenadierspoort**, built around the **Ridderzaal** (Knights Hall) which is used for combined parliamentary sessions of the lower and upper houses; the opening of parliament; and important state functions.

Government offices surround one of Holland's greatest art museums, the **Mauritshuis** which is situated close to the Plein and next to the Vijver ornamental lake. Built between 1633 and 1644 by Pieter Post, it was Holland's first Italian-classic structure. The royal picture collection was moved here in 1821 and forms the nucleus of what you will see here today. Among the works on show are those by Rembrandt, Hals and Jan Steen.

The Hague is a city of many great museums including the **Mesdag**, 7 Laan van Meerdervoort, where there are good examples of modern Dutch painters along with works by Corot, Daubigny and Rousseau. (Open daily 1000–1700, Sun. from 1300.) In the **Gemeentemuseum** (Municipal Museum) there are old musical instruments and art by Mondriaan whilst in the **Bredius Museum**, there are more Old Masters. Other suggestions include the **Costume Museum**, the **Poster Museum**, the **Museum for Education** and the **National Automobile Museum**. **Gevangenpoort** is also a museum, now containing a collection of torture instruments. The building is in fact Holland's oldest prison (14th-century) whose 'guests' included the De Witt brothers. (A statue of Johan De Witt stands on the Plaats).

At 65b Zee Straat, there is a gigantic circular painting called the **Panorama Mesdag**, painted by H.W. Mesdag. Measuring 14m/45ft high and 122m/400ft in circumference, it depicts the adjacent resort of Scheveningen. (Open daily from 1000 to mid afternoon.) Opposite the Mesdag Museum is the **Vredespaleis** (Peace Palace) where the permanent Court of Arbitration, the International Court of Justice and the Academy of International Law, sit. Built in a romantic Flemish style from a plan submitted by Louis Cordonnier of Lille in an architectural competition, it was constructed with a $1.5 million contribution from Scottish-American steel tycoon, Andrew Carnegie. More than 30 countries donated the furniture and furnishings. (Open daily from 1000–1200 and 1400–1600; Sun. 1400–1600).

The **Huis Ten Bosch** is the home of Queen Beatrix and her family. If the royal flag is flying, the Queen is in residence, but the palace cannot be visited.

The Gothic **Town Hall** (1564) is in Gravenstraat. Nearby, the **Church of St Jacob** (14th-century) boasts a lovely 15th-century pulpit and the arms of the Knights of the Golden Fleece. One of The Hague's greatest attractions, however, is the miniature town of **Madurodam**. On the southern side of one of the canals connecting The Hague to Scheveningen it is a composite representation of many of Holland's cities. Everything is on a scale of 1/25th life size and is very detailed including a harbour with light house, quayside with ferries, airport, trains, amusement parks, barges and windmills – and everything works. When it gets dark, lights go on in the homes, streets are illuminated and the medieval castles are floodlit.

The Hague is a smart city with plenty of elegant hotels, restaurants and shops. Night life centres on the Lange Houtstraat although on summer evenings, many tourists go to lively Scheveningen nearby. *Amsterdam 60km/37.5mi; Rotterdam 26km/16mi.*

Madurodam

Den Helder   C8

(pop. 61,000) Since the 18th century this has become Holland's main naval base and training centre. The British and French fleets were defeated here in 1673 by Van Tromp and De Ruyter. In 1795, the ice-bound Dutch fleet was captured by a French cavalry detachment. Apart from the fleet and an aquarium, there is little else to see in Den Helder, but there are beaches at **Huisduinen**, a 15-minute bus ride away. *Texel* (largest of the west Frisian Islands) *3km/2mi.*

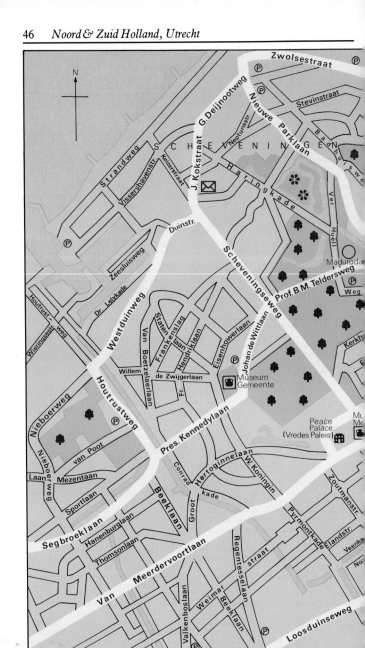

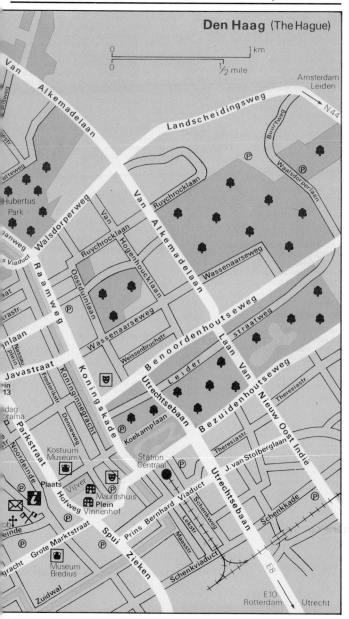

Den Haag (The Hague)

0 _____ 1 km
0 _____ ½ mile

Amsterdam
Leiden

N44

Van
Alkemadelaan

Landscheidingsweg

Buurtweg

Waalsdorperlaan

Hubertus
Park

Walsdorperweg

Ruychrocklaan

Van Hogenhoucklaan

Van Alkemadelaan

Wassenaarseweg

Raamweg

Oostduinlaan

Ruychrocklaan

Wassenaarseweg

Weissenbruchstr.

Benoordenhoutseweg

Leider straatweg

Laan Van

s Viaduct

Nassau
plein

Javastraat

in
13

Parkstraat

Noordeinde

Frederikstr.

Koninginnegracht

Denneweg

Utrechtsebaan

Koekamplaan

Bezuidenhoutseweg

Nieuw Oost Indië

Utrechtsebaan

Theresiastr.

Theresiastr.

J. van Stolberglaan

Schenkkade

Kostuum
Museum

Plaats

Vijver

Hofweg

Mauritshuis

Plein
Binnenhof

Station
Centraal

Prins Bernhard Viaduct

Schenkweg

Lekstr.

Grote Marktstraat

Spui

Zieken

Maasstr.

Schenkviaduct

E8

Museum
Bredius

Zuidwal

E10
Rotterdam   Utrecht

Hillegom   K7

(pop. 16,000) A town in the middle of the bulb growing area, on the main road from Haarlem to Leiden. Visit **Treslong Gardens** (admission free), the official demonstration garden for bulb growers, started in 1949. Bulb auctions are held in spring on Thursdays in the Exchange here. In the warehouses, you can watch the bulbs prepared and packed for export. The April **Bloemencorso** (flower parade) takes place on the third or fourth Sunday morning and often starts from here. *Amsterdam 30km/19mi.*

Hilversum   L11

(pop. 93,000) A modern city with striking architecture, wide tree-lined streets and pedestrian-zoned squares. The plans were the work of W.M. Dudok and its buildings are so unusual that even the town hall resembles a luxury hotel. Hilversum is the home of the Dutch radio and television network and an excellent base for exploring the **Het Gooi** region. By the nearby **Loosdrecht Lakes** there is golfing, riding, tennis, sailing and rowing. *Amsterdam 34km/21mi.*

Hook of Holland   O3

(pop. 8,000) A port at the mouth of the new waterway. Anyone who is fascinated by shipping will enjoy this busy city, watching sea traffic sail in and out of Rotterdam. It is also a family resort with a wide, quiet beach, children's playground, a few simple amusements and a large forest nearby. *Rotterdam 25km/16mi.*

Hoorn   G10

(pop. 25,000) Once an important harbour town made rich by 17th-century East Indies trade, but when the harbour silted up in the 18th century, it declined. The harbour is still picturesque. One of its remaining old gateways, the tower of **Hoofdtoren**, built in brick and stone in 1532, became the offices of Hoorn's whaling fleet. The town was the birthplace of Willem Cornelis Schouten (1580–1625) who was the first explorer to go round the tip of South America, naming it Cape Horn in 1616. Other famous natives include Jan Pieterszoon Coen (1587–1629), founder of what is now Djakarta; and Abel Janszoon Tasman (1602–59), the navigator who gave his name to the island of Tasmania.

Walk through Hoorn and you'll see plenty of rich architecture, including 17th-century warehouses, gateways and merchants' mansions. Houses on Grote Costraat in particular are elaborately decorated. At the bottom of this is the 15th-century **Oosterkerk** with 17th-century stained glass and close by is the 16th-century **Oosterpoort** with its attractive canal bridge. Follow the gardens and you'll come to the **House of 1624**, now a small museum. The **West Frisian Museum** (housed in the Staten College dating from 1632) mirrors the town's former glory with a miscellany of paintings, antiques and historic items. (Open 1000–1700 daily, Sun. 1200–1700). Walk along the Kleine Noord stretching from the Brede to the **Noorderkerk** (1441). Other fine architectural examples are the Kerkpleins 16th-century **St John's Hospital** and the 17th-century **Town Hall**.

A statue of Jan Coen stands on the main square, the Rode Steen, where a Dutch market with handicrafts and folk dances is held every Wednesday from mid June to mid August between 0900–1700. From May–Aug. a steam train runs from Hoorn to Medemblik. *Medemblik 15km/9mi.*

IJmuiden   I7

(pop. 38,000) The Netherlands' largest fishing harbour with impressive sea lock installations at the entrance of the 24km/15mi canal connecting it to Amsterdam. The canal allows ships up to 105,000 tons to pass through it on their way to and from the capital. Fish are auctioned off from the enormous trawler fleet at a 610m/2000ft fish market.

There is a wide ocean beach at nearby **Velsen** and the lovely **Velserbeek** park – two of the reasons this is a weekend retreat for Amsterdamers.

Katwijk   L5

(pop. 38,000) A bright beach resort, a 30-minute tram ride from Leiden. There are plenty of cafes, shops and entertainments, especially in summer. The beach is backed by a promenade and the town is surrounded by woods and dunes. Boat trips on the **Kager Lakes** are possible. *Amsterdam 44km/27.5mi.*

Kinderdijk   P7

An area in the Alblasserwaard district, half way between Rotterdam and Dordrecht at the meeting point of the rivers Nieuwe Maas, Lek and Noord. It is renowned for its windmills, 19 of which continue to operate. Their sails are set in motion every Saturday during July and August. From April to the end of September (save Sundays), at least one of the mills is open daily and can be inspected. Inside there is a stove and concealed closet beds. This area began

Kinderdijk

to be reclaimed in the 10th century. Many streams and rivers run through it and you'll notice houses built on top of dykes for flood protection. Kinderdijk may easily be reached by bus or train from Rotterdam. *Rotterdam 15km/9mi.*

Leiden   M6

(pop. 103,000) Holland's oldest university town, Leiden, began as a Roman settlement, and rose to become an important textile centre in the 14th century. Besieged by Spain in 1574, Leiden held out stoically for a year until saved by William The Silent who ordered the dykes to be cut for the Dutch fleet to sail over the flooded polders. As thanks for their bravery, the citizens were given the choice of a tax remission or a university. They chose the latter which was founded in 1575, so that by the 17th century, it had become a famous teaching centre.

Right in the middle of town is the **Burcht**, a 12th-century artificial mound with a fortress on top. Around this focal point there is a maze of narrow streets and alleyways, crossing the many canals. Across the Rapenburg canal is the **University** (16th-century). The old building, a former convent, now houses a museum; the **Botanical Gardens** behind also date from the 16th century. Take Nieuwstraat to reach the 15th-century **Hooglandsekerk** with little houses along its walls and the tomb of Van der Werff, inside. The city's greatest church, **Pieterskerk**, which took over 300

years to build, can be reached via the Papengracht. A plaque on the baptistry wall commemorates the Pilgrim Fathers and their pastor, John Robinson, who was prevented by ill health from going with them to America in 1620. He, along with Jan Steen are among those buried in the church. See also the nearby old **Gravenstein** prison (13th–17th centuries) and the **Town Hall** (17th century) on the lively main thoroughfare of Breestraat.

Rembrandt was born in Leiden and a number of his paintings can be seen in the **Lakenhal Museum**, 28 Oude Singel, a museum built originally as a cloth hall in 1639. In addition to the art and silver exhibits, there is a variety of items relating to Leiden's history and siege. (Open daily 1000–1700, Sun. 1300–1700). Other good museums include the **Rijksmuseum van Oudheden** at Rapenburg 28 with its outstanding Egyptian, Roman, Greek and prehistoric antiquities; the **Ethnological Museum** with its Buddha room and the **Science Museum** and the **De Valk Windmill Museum**. *Amsterdam 40km/25mi.*

Lisse   K6

(pop. 20,000) A town in the middle of Holland's bulb belt, most famous for the

Keukenhof Gardens

Keukenhof Gardens. The flower exhibition held here from late March to mid-May is known all over the world. (Open 0800–2000, but remember the gardens get very crowded at this time of year.) Holland's largest hyacinth fields (best seen in early April) are at **Veenenburgerlaan** between Lisse and Hillegom. *Amsterdam 34km/21mi.*

Marken   I10

(pop. 1700) Once an island, Marken was built on stilts because of the danger from flooding. Today a dyke road connects it to the mainland or it may be reached by a 25-minute boat ride from Monnickendam or neighbouring Volendam. The village is typical of old Holland and the residents wear their own national costume. The women wear red and white bodices covered by bright, sleeveless fronts, dark skirts, and a small embroidered lace cap sometimes held in place by a ribbon under the chin. The men wear blue blouses and baggy linen knee breeches under red belts. Children under five are dressed alike with one exception — both wear skirts, the difference is, the boys' skirts are blue! *Amsterdam 22km/14mi.*

Medemblik   E11

(pop. 6000) The oldest town in the province of Noord-Holland and another important 17th-century Zuider Zee trading centre. Until Hoorn took over, this was the major town in the west of Friesland where the Frisian royal family ruled from **Radboud Castle** (built about 700). What you can see today – brick and slate paths surrounded by moats – dates from the 13th century. Lord George Murray (who fought alongside Bonnie Prince Charlie at Culloden in 1746) lived and died in exile in Medemblik and his tomb is in the **St Bonifaciuskerk** (15th-century). The old-fashioned steam train journey from Hoorn to Medemblik in May–Aug. is worth taking.
Hoorn 19km/12mi.

Monnickendam   I10

(pop. 9500) A pretty little town with a history dating back to 1355 when it acquired its city charter. East India trade and easy access to Amsterdam made the town wealthy in the 17th century. The 18th-century **Town Hall** has a **Speeltoren** (bell tower) which dates from the 16th century and whose carillon features a procession of clockwork knights when the hour chimes. The old **Waag** (weigh house) stands on the waterfront, and the **Museum Stuttenburgh** has displays of music boxes and mechanical musical instruments. Monnickendam is also well-known for its eel-smoking houses.
Amsterdam 15km/9mi.

Naarden   K11

(pop. 19,500) The Netherlands' best preserved fortress town, dating back to 1350 when it was built to defend an expanding Amsterdam. Although considered impregnable, it was captured in 1572 by Don Frederick of Toledo who murdered most of its inhabitants. Its star-shaped moats and ramparts still exist and the **Grote Kerk** has such good acoustics that it attracts many a visitor on Good Friday to hear *St Matthew Passion. Amsterdam 25km/15.5mi.*

Noordwijk aan Zee   L5

(pop. 20,000) A cosmopolitan seaside resort situated in the flower-growing district west of Lisse and one which is a sports and entertainment centre. The main street, Koningin Wilhemina Boulevard, runs right along the sea front, the beach to one side, a string of hotels to the other. A small charge is made for using the beach where a lifeguard watches out for children.

In Noordwijk you will find all the amenities you'd expect to find in a modern resort. There are good shops, children's amusements, chic cafes and lots of sporting activities including fresh or salt water swimming, water skiing, sailing, tennis, bowling and horse riding.

The town's modern arcaded square has fountains, seats and shops and is overlooked by a white lighthouse. The resort's residential section is Noordwijk Binnen, 3km/2mi away. This is a very popular destination with people coming from Amsterdam, Haarlem, Leiden and The Hague. *Amsterdam 40km/25mi.*

Oudewater   N9

(pop. 7000) A town located between Gouda and Utrecht, notorious for its persecution of witches. Anyone who was suspected of being a witch was brought to the Weigh House, dressed in a paper witch's costume, and weighed in front of the mayor, aldermen and weigh master. Anyone who weighed more than 45kg/99lbs got a certificate to prove it – obviously too heavy to ride a broomstick! Anyone who weighed less than that was killed by fire or drowned in the nearest canal. Between May and September, you can still get weighed here and receive that certificate. If you do happen to be lighter than 45kg/99lbs., it's still OK – times have changed and they'll let you fly away!

Oudewater is a pleasant town with a number of pretty gabled houses and warehouses flanking quiet canals. Worth noting are the 13th-century saddle-backed tower of **St Michael's Church** and the **Hallenkerk** with its barrel vaults. The 16th-century **Town Hall** contains some interesting paintings including one showing a massacre by the Duke of Alva's troops.
Rotterdam 37km/23mi.

Rotterdam O6

(pop. 582,000) The world's largest seaport and Holland's second city situated on the estuaries of the Mass (Meuse) and the Rhine making it one of Europe's major trading centres. Since it was almost completely destroyed during the last war, the city you see today is an ultra modern one. There are plenty of pedestrian-zoned shopping precincts like the flower and statue decorated **Lijnbaan**; cafes, restaurants and smart hotels, many centred on the Stationsplein and around the Coolsingel – so the atmosphere is a very continental one.
What to see Climb the 183m/600ft **Euromast** for a panoramic view of the city. There is a platform at 31m/102ft and, at 91m/300ft, a bar, coffee shop and restaurant. A revolving, glass-encased capsule takes visitors up to the Space Tower at the top of the Euromast. Pleasure cruisers will take you right through the heart of the dock area from the Willemsplein landing stage.

Rotterdam's Euromast

These boats tour the port area and leave every 45 minutes in spring and summer and at one and a half hourly intervals for the rest of the year.
Boymans-van Beuningen Museum, Mathenesserlaan 18, houses a vast collection of sculptures, ceramics, furnishings and paintings by Hals, Rembrandt, Steen and Van Gogh. Two others worth seeing are the **Museum of Ethnology**, Willemskade 25 and **Professor van der Poel Tax Museum**, Parklaan 14–16.

An outing to **Delfshaven** is a must. Once it was a town in its own right but now it is incorporated into the city. It's a small tranquil district where 16th-century houses doze by a quiet lagoon, much favoured by artists. It was from this spot that the Pilgrim Fathers first left for America in 1620.
Where to stay There's a good choice of hotels in all categories from the recommended Atlanta to the well-known Hilton.
Eating out A wide choice in all categories.
Amsterdam 76km/47.5mi.

Scheveningen M4

(pop. 38,000) A vivacious beach resort on The Hague's doorstep with a cosmopolitan atmosphere. Among its best features are the casino (western Europe's largest) which is to be found in the completely renovated **Kurhaus**, now a hotel but dating from 1885 – it offers roulette and black jack at 24 tables. Another feature is the **Wave Pool**, a recreation centre under glass, which has a whirlpool; indoor and outdoor pools; saunas; solariums; and sports rooms. (Open May–Sept. 1000–2300 daily; Oct.–Apr. Mon.–Fri. 1400–2200; weekends, 0100–2200.)

Lively Scheveningen can offer eating places to suit all budgets, boutiques, amusements and all kinds of sport amenities. Something is always going on here in summer from art exhibitions to firework displays. Much of the action takes place around the pier which links four artificial 'islands', combining a fun park with shopping arcade, bars and look-out tower. Deep sea fishing is available for a small fee from the Fishing Ring and there is also a cycling track.
The Hague 7km/4mi.

Schiedam P5

(pop. 75,000) A bustling town of waterways and shipyards adjoining Rotterdam. It used to be Europe's greatest gin-producing city with over 300 gin distilleries on the banks of the Schie River. A number of those still exist and a National Distillery Museum in the **Municipal Museum** is worth seeing. The museum mansion was built in the 18th century by Jan Guidici.

Another liquor-oriented collection is the **De Jongh**, Lange Haven 74. It comprises some 5000 miniature bottles made from all kinds of materials including wood and is one of the largest and most valuable collections in the world. (Open Tues.–Thurs. 1030–1600).

See also the 17th-century **Town Hall**, the 15th-century **Grotekerk**, 18th-century warehouses and patrician houses, and the world's highest windmill, **De Walvisch**, one of four in the area.

Schoonhoven   O8

(pop. 11,000) A charming old town on the
River Lek, best known for its silver works.
The **Gold, Silver and Clock Museum** at 7
Haven pays tribute to the remarkable skills
of Schoonhoven's traditional craftsmen.
Wander through Schoonhoven and you'll
see the 17th-century **Veerpoort** gateway on
the river; the **Weigh House** (1617) and the
16th-century **Municipal Corn House**
where grain was kept as a reserve for use in
times of trouble.

In the 15th-century **Town Hall** museum
there are bells cast from guns taken from
the first Dutch ship to sail round the world
(1598). The tomb of explorer Olivier van
Noort, who sailed in that ship, is in the
Gothic 14th-century **Hallenkerk**, along
with that of Klass Blom who introduced
windmills to Spain in 1547. The surrounding countryside is very typical of Zuid-
Holland. *Rotterdam 28km/17.5mi.*

Spaarndam   J7

A residential suburb of Haarlem well
known for its statue of Pieter, fictional hero
of the American book, *Hans Brinker* or *The
Silver Skates* – the boy who saved Haarlem
by putting his finger in the dyke. A small
monument to this popular story book figure
was unveiled by Princess Irene in 1950.
Spaarndam is also the place where Frans
Hals married for the second time in 1617.
Amsterdam 18km/11mi.

Texel   A8

(pop. 11,000) The largest and most southerly of the West Frisian Islands, which may
be reached in 15 minutes by ferry from Den
Helder. Between May and June, this island
is a bird paradise with hundreds of species
breeding here. Special guides take visitors
to the nesting area. With its sandy beaches
and unspoilt countryside, Texel attracts
many visitors, especially during the summer months. The main resort is **De Koog**
on the west coast.

Utrecht   M11

(pop. 236,000) Capital of Utrecht Province
and fourth largest city in the Netherlands,
Utrecht has been a Roman fortress, a
Franconian citadel and a church mission
station. The War of Spanish Succession was
ended by the *Treaty of Utrecht* (1713) signed
in the university chapter hall. Today, the
city pleasantly combines old and new and
trade fairs and exhibitions have trans-
formed Utrecht into an international busi-
ness centre.

Canals in the old city centre have quays
giving access to cellars. The **Domkerk** on
Domplein, begun in 1254 was only finally
finished 300 years later. Its 112m/367ft
Dom Tower was separated from the
cathedral when the nave collapsed in a
storm in 1674. While never rebuilt, the
remains are impressive, including
monumental tombs, stained-glass windows
and 15th-century wall painting. It is connected to the **University** (founded in 1636)
by an attractive cloister passage. The University Chapter Hall is open daily 0900–
1200 and 1400–1700; closed Sat. afternoons
and Sun.

There are several interesting Roman and
Gothic churches such as **St Pieterskerk**,
behind the cathedral, which has frescoes
and an unusual crypt, or the **Paushuis** on
Kromme Nieuwe Gracht (1523) which
commemorates Holland's only Pope,
Adrian VI.

There are also *hofjes* and patrician
houses like **Bartholomeus Gasthuis** in
Lange Smeestraat which contains magnifi-
cent Gobelin tapestries. See also **St Cather-
ine's Convent** which tells the story of
Dutch Christianity. The **Central Museum**,
Agnietenstraat 1, has good collections of
paintings, furnishings and costumes.
(Open daily 1000–1700; Sun. 1400–1700.)
See, too, the **Netherlands Railway
Museum**, 6 Johan van Oldenbarneveltlaan.
Amsterdam 36km/22.5mi.

Volendam   I10

(pop. 13,000) A fishing village noted for its
colourful costumes, it is reached along the
old sea dyke from Monnickendam or
Edam. The men wear baggy black trousers,
long sleeveless waistcoats fastened with silver buttons, and round black caps. Women
wear striped skirts with aprons over them,
winged lace bonnets unless they are in an
older age bracket in which case they may
wear black caps to attend church. The best
time to photograph them is on a Sunday
morning. The village also specializes in
fried or smoked eel and there are many
cheese farms in the area where visitors can
watch the old method of making and
moulding cheeses.
Amsterdam 20km/12.5mi.

Zandvoort   J6

(pop. 16,000) A large North Sea resort
which was flattened when the Germans
built the Atlantic Wall. It has since been
rebuilt completely and boasts a number of
big hotels, shops etc. along its 3km/2mi
promenade. There is an 18-hole golf course
here, camp sites, motor racing circuit,
open-air swimming pools and wooded
dunes for walkers. *Amsterdam 29km/18mi.*

ZEELAND

Situated in the southwest of the Netherlands, Zeeland is a region of large sea-arms, lakes and groups of islands linked to the mainland by dams and bridges. Fishing and farming are the main sources of income for the Zeeland people, most of whom live on those islands in the deltas of the Waal and Scheldt.

The province has a pleasant landscape – a mixture of beaches, woods, dunes and polders scattered with interesting villages and historic towns. A charming district not without its own local colour as can be seen on market days in places like Middelburg and Goes when residents wear traditional costume. These and other lovely towns like Veere and Zierikzee all recall the province's great days before silt ruined its harbours in the 17th century and trading prosperity left the cities of the Zuider Zee.

Zeeland is a marvellous place for sports enthusiasts. Its flat areas are ideal for cyclists; its lakes and rivers admirable for sailing, water skiing and wind surfing.

Shrimps and oysters Zeeland is *the* place for oysters, usually served in their natural state. Shrimp and lobster are both on many menus and for a quickie snack, try eels on a bun. Sea snails and salt spinnach are also Zeeland dishes. Look, too, for *boterbabbelaars*, a type of sweet.

Festivals and events July: tilting the ring contest on horseback in Vlissingen. Summer music festivals in Middelburg.

Beveland   D5 E5

North and South Beveland were islands before the Delta Plan linked them to Walcheren. The local people wear distinctive costume and that, together with the area's farms, orchards and windmills gives the suggestion of 'Holland in miniature'.

Goes   D6

(pop. 31,000) A town at the centre of a rich fruit-growing area in South Beveland. Tuesday is market day when the residents dress in their traditional costume. Women wear distinctive winged lace bonnets, for example. Most of the memorable and historic buildings, and several good hotels, are situated in the main square. The major one of note is the **Grotekerk**, dedicated to Mary Magdalene (1427), with some beautiful windows and an ancient organ. Also worth a look is the **Town Hall** for its fine iron work and stucco decorations in Louis XV style. Gabled houses line the Turfkade around the market and harbour area.

Goes is a good base for touring the Bevelands as there is a frequent bus service to other small towns and villages in its vicinity. An old-fashioned steam train also leaves here for South Beveland. *Middelburg 22km/ 14mi.*

Middelburg   E4

(pop. 38,000) The capital of Zeeland Province, situated on Walcheren a few miles north of Vlissingen and easily reached by bus from there. A defensive fortress was built here in the 9th century and in the Middle Ages Middelburg rivalled Bruges for its wealthy wool trade.

The Gothic **Town Hall**, one of Holland's most beautiful, dates from the 15th century. Later additions (early 16th century) were the tower and the meat hall, now an exhibition centre. The 12th-century Abbey was burnt down in 1940 but has since been rebuilt as the **Zeeland Museum**. You can climb its 85m/285ft tower, nicknamed Lange Jan (Long John) for a view over the district. It has a good carillon and in summer there are *son et lumière* presentations here.

Also see the 13th-century **Koorkerk** and the 16th-century **Nieuwekerk**, both restored after wartime damage. Some of the surviving old gates include the **Kuiperspoort** (1586) surrounded by old warehouses; the **Gistpoort** (1509) and the **Koepoort** (1735). Until 1787, the **Kloveniersdoelen** (1607) was used by the civil guard.

On Thursday, market day, like so many other towns in this province, the local ladies wear splendid costumes when they bring their produce to town. In the north of town,

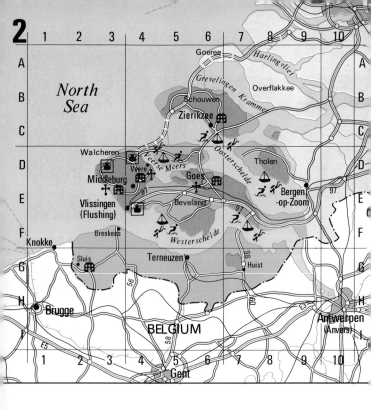

by the Koepoort is **Miniatuur Walcheren**, a scaled model of the town planted with 100,000 dwarf trees and shrubs and 200 models on a ½0th scale, including turning windmills, ships, houses, churches, trains and barges. (Open daily from around the beginning of April to the end of September.) In July and August, the town organizes a Youth Centre facility where families may leave young children during the day. *Rotterdam 106km/66mi.*

Schouwen-Duiveland   B6 C7

A small island, good for a quiet holiday with its green fields, dunes, sandy beaches and quaint villages. It is also home to a host of birds of many species.

Sluis   G2

(pop. 3000) Formerly an important seaport on the now silted up Zwin, located only 3km/2mi from the Belgian border. In 1340 here, Edward III sank or captured 166 ships from a 200-strong French fleet, and in 1587 the town was besieged by the Spanish.

The 1944 bombing killed a number of its inhabitants and destroyed much of the town but it has since been rebuilt. The Flemish **Town Hall** (14th-century) contains Holland's only belfry. The city walls have three gates and there is an 18th-century corn mill still in use. The weekly Friday market is always a popular attraction.

Veere   D4

(pop. 4200) A delightful small town which once boasted a population of 20,000 during the 15th century. At the peak of its power when it handled woollen imports from Scotland, a monopoly was given to Wolfert van Borselen who married Mary Stuart, daughter of Scotland's James I. It was the Borselen family who built the **Town Hall** in 1474. The large, Gothic **Grote Kerk** contains the tombs of Mary Stuart and her Dutch husband. Dating from the 15th century, the church was restored after a fire in 1686 and later served as a hospital for Napoleon's troops. Opposite the church is the Stadsfontein, a clear water well given in

1551 by Maximilian of Burgundy to the Scottish merchants who had requested clean water to wash their wool. The **De Schotse Huizen** (Scottish house) **Museum** contains old maps, costumes, wrought iron and Ming china. The Delta Scheme turned the sea channel separating Veere from North Beveland into the freshwater Veerse Meer, a holiday marina. *Middelburg 8km/ 5mi.*

Vlissingen (Flushing)   E3

(pop. 45,000) A popular summer family resort and well-known harbour town at the mouth of Westerschelde. With direct access to the North Sea, Vlissingen has been an important seaport since the Middle Ages. It is still a busy ship building centre as you can see when you walk along its boulevard. This boulevard, named Evertsen, high above the water, is lined with hotels, shops, cafes and restaurants. There is a statue of the Dutch sea hero, Michiel de Ruyter, who was born here, and the **Stedelijk Museum** in Bellamy Park has a collection of model ships among other things.

Of historic interest are the 14th-century church in the market and the 16th-century town gate, **Westerport**. Ferries run between here and Breskens across the Scheldt if you wish to explore the 64km/40mi stretch of Flanders.

Walcheren   D3

Formerly an island in the Scheldt estuary, it is now joined to North and South Beveland. Lying as it does below sea level, it has always been in danger of flooding. In October 1944, the RAF broke the dykes at Westkapelle, Vlissingen, Veere and Rammekens in order to free Antwerp from the Germans. Walcheren stayed under water for over a year until drainage was completed in 1946. The 1953 floods were another disaster from which Walcheren has happily recovered.

Zierikzee   C6

(pop. 9500) A harbour town full of charm on Schouwen-Duiveland, reputed to be one of the best preserved in the Netherlands. It was founded in 848 and the spired tower of the harbour gateway (15th-century) gives it the appearance of a citadel. There are several elaborately gabled houses and a colourful fish market here, but the greatest attraction is the **Tower of Sint Lievens Monster-toren**. It was planned to be 207m/680ft high but money ran out when it was only 60m/197ft. However, its belfry still commands the area. *Middelburg 45km/28mi.*

NOORD BRABANT

In many ways, Noord Brabant resembles Belgium, immediately to the south, for the majority of people here are Roman Catholic and like the Belgian Brabant people, love their food and celebrations. Carnival here is one of the year's liveliest occasions celebrated with much fervour.

It is a region with large forests, nature reserves, asparagus fields and farms. The villages on its moors were sketched by Van Gogh, but today this is a popular province with self-caterers.

Pumpernickel and pea soup The carnival lovers of Noord Brabant opt for anything that is good for a hangover. Dutch pea soup is the dish here as is the local pumpernickel. Sausage bread is another favourite food in this province.

Festivals and events Summer handicraft festivals. May: music festivals. June: jazz in Bergen-op-zoom. Aug.: jazz in Breda.

Bergen-op-Zoom   F1

(pop. 43,000) An ancient fortified town, seat of viscounts, located on the road to Zeeland at the head of a short canal leading to the Scheldt. It was a particularly wealthy centre in the Middle Ages and today is an important vegetable and oyster centre, with a pleasant shopping area in the old quarter and a modern yacht haven.

Among the buildings of note are the **Grotekerk of St Gertrude**; the 15th-century **Town Hall** with its imposing façade of 1611; the **Gevangenenpoort** or prisoners' gate (c. 14th-century), a relic of the town's medieval fortifications; and the

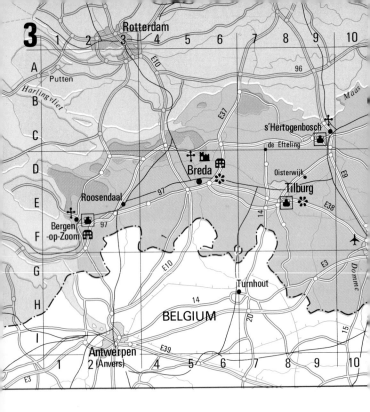

3

Rotterdam

A

Putten

Harlingvliet

B

C

s'Hertogenbosch

de Efteling

D

Breda

Oisterwijk

Tilburg

Roosendaal

97

E

E38

Bergen
-op-Zoom

97

F

G

Turnhout

H

BELGIUM

I

Antwerpen
(Anvers)

Maas

E9

E3

Domme

Marquis' Court which is now the Municipal Museum. There are many well-restored old houses inside the fortified city and beside the old harbour. *Goes 40km/25mi.*

Breda   E5

(pop. 119,000) The town where the English and Dutch signed the peace treaty under which New Amsterdam became English and changed its name to New York. It was the old seat of the Counts of Nassau and it passed from the Spanish to the Dutch in the 17th century then to the French in 1795 who held it until 1813.

As an example of the emergence of Brabant, look at the Gothic-styled **Church of our Lady**. A similar style can be seen on statues placed above grave-stones in the area. The church has a beautiful carillon tower 97m/318ft high; some interesting tombs and a 16th-century triptych. The **Begijnhof** (almshouses surrounding a tiny lawn) in Catherinastraat are the only ones in Holland still occupied by *beguines* (lay sisters).

Breda Castle, rebuilt in 1536 on 12th-century foundations, is now the Royal Military Academy (access may be arranged by the VVV office in Breda). King Charles II stayed here in 1660 during his exile, after his defeat by Cromwell. The Breda Military Tattoo takes place here for ten days at the end of August. The castle garden, **Valkenberg Park**, is laid out with fountains, lawns, pergolas, flower-beds and rare-trees, but there are several other notable parks besides this one, notably **Wilhelmina** and **Sonsbeek**. The **Vleeshal** (17th-century meat hall) is now the Municipal and Episcopal Museum.

On Saturday mornings between April and September, an antiques and art market is held in the historic **Havermalkt** market. In the nearby village of **Zundert**, on the first Sunday in September, an elaborate flower festival takes place. Breda has plenty of shops, hotels and entertainment and is linked by good motorways to Utrecht, Rotterdam and Eindhoven making it an excellent touring centre. *Rotterdam 52km/ 32.5mi.*

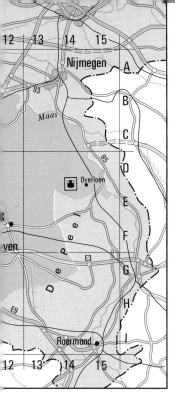

12 13 14 15
Nijmegen A
93
Maas B
C
D
Overloon
E
ven F
E3
G
D H
E9
Roermond I
12 13 14 15

s'Hertogenbosch   C9

(pop. 90,000) The town is built around an attractive market place and dominated by one of the Netherlands' finest Gothic cathedrals, **St Janskerk** (14th-century), which rises in the shape of a Latin cross and is just as impressive inside with a five-arched nave resting on 150 ornate pillars. A 48-bell carillon plays every Wednesday for an hour at noon and its 17th-century carved organ, one of Holland's largest, was installed under John Bull's direction. (He was said to have composed the British National Anthem.) The 17th-century **Town Hall** has its own 38-bell carillon with moving figures and inside, paintings by some of the Dutch Masters.

The **Lieve Vreow Brotherhood**, Hinthamerstraat 94, is Holland's oldest religious order, founded in 1318, whose museum houses maps, pewter and antiques. The **Noordbrabants Museum** at Bethaniestraat 4 covers the history and culture of the province. (Open Tues.–Fri. 1000–1700; Sat., Sun. and public holidays 1300–1700). Hieronymus Bosch, the 15th-century painter, was born in s'Hertogenbosch and his statue stands in the market place surrounded by old gabled houses. *Eindhoven 35km/22mi.*

Overloon   D14

(pop. 3500) A village next to the 300ha/740acre nature area – the Overloon Dunes. The latter was obliterated in October 1944 by a 100,000 shell barrage, followed by a tank battle which lasted ten days and ended with 300 wrecked tanks. The **International Peace Museum** (Holland's largest war museum) was opened with the assistance of the allied military authorities as a memorial to this event. Close by the 16ha/40acre park which houses this is the **IJsselsteyn** German war cemetery with the graves of 30,000 German soldiers who died in the area. *s'Hertogenbosch 72km/45mi.*

Tilburg   E8

(pop. 160,000) Once an important textile town but currently well known for the many wine importers who have vast cellars here. As a reminder of the textile industry, the Netherlands' **Textile Museum** is worth visiting.

One of Europe's most unusual recreation parks, **De Efteling** is only 11km/7mi north, just before Kaatsheuvel. Covering 152ha/376acres, it is combination of playground, picnic site and amusement area with puppet theatres, restaurants, boating and swimming, miniature railways and fairytale castles.

Eindhoven   F11

(pop. 196,000) This model industrial city, known as 'the city of light', is the headquarters of Philips Electric Company, founded by Anton Philips, the great Dutch industrialist. Until 80 years ago, it was a sleepy community – then the villages in the area merged to become one giant electrical centre.

Eindhoven is also internationally known for its **Abbe Museum**, Bilderdijklaan 10, which has some first rate modern artworks by painters like Picasso. (Open Tues.–Sat. 1000–1700; Sun. and holidays, 1300–1700.) Also see **Evoluon**, la Noordbrabantlaan, a museum that combines science and architecture, almost an adult toy showing man's ingenuity and technical development – you need at least two hours to see it. (Open Mon.–Fri. 0930–1730; Sat. 1000–1700; Sun. and holidays, 1200–1700.) Near the Evoluon is the 50hectare/125acre **Eurostrand**, a recreational beach and sports centre with bathing, rowing, camping and restaurant facilities. *Venlo 61km/38mi.*

GRONINGEN FRIESLAND DRENTHE

It is the sea which gives the northern part of the Netherlands its looks and character – and always has. The sea has been held back by dykes, and land has been reclaimed to join former islands with the mainland. Groningen, Friesland and Drenthe are all green provinces, areas brightened by meers, waterways and old dreamy towns where windmill sails still turn. This is farming country and everywhere you'll see enormous single-roofed farmsteads. For the sportsman, especially the boating enthusiast, these are regions of great interest.

Thanks to the water, the land is fertile so that the black and white Frisian cattle are highly regarded the world over. The province only has one large town, Leeuwarden, and that is supported by the dairy industry. It is an area of state forests, tranquil lakes and offshore islands, whose seamen's cafes are known far beyond Holland's borders. The Gaasterland district is ideal for biking and cycling and horseback riding may be enjoyed all over.

Before there were dykes, there were *wierds* or earth mounds on which villages were built for protection against tidal floods. You can see them in Groningen and in Friesland, where they are called *terps*. Groningen, which is best known for its *borgen* (fortified estates), its medieval chapels and windmills, has a similar appearance to Friesland, but its peat bogs and sandy soil run across to Drenthe, the Netherlands' least known and least populated province. It was Groningen folk who invented the *wadlopen*, low water dikes over the tidal flats between the mainland and the offshore Wadden islands.

Drenthe may not have many people, but it can boast of a new prosperity – from the oil fields and gas pockets, discovered not long ago. An ancient heritage can be found here, too – the *hunebedden* or prehistoric graves. Many, many moons ago, the inhabitants of this area used to pile heavy stones upon their graves. The resulting structure was soon covered with earth and overgrown with grass, so that the *hunebedden* simulated little hills. (Many of Drenthe's fifty three *hunebedden* are in the Hondsrug district.)

These three northern provinces with their dunes and woodlands, their water and their rustic qualities have become known as 'one of the great green lungs of all Holland'.

Stews and cakes The people in the northern provinces are hearty eaters and love stews. You'll find lots of different kinds, especially in Groningen. As for cakes, this is the region to come to. Try *Groningen koek* and *Oude wijven* and certainly in Drenthe, the *kruidcake*, a spicy sweetmeat or *Drentse stoek*, a sort of currant cake. Sweet things don't always have to stay on the dessert trolley – the Dutch tend to use syrup with savouries. *Pagast*, for example (which you'll find in Drenthe) is, believe it or not, a thick groat mixture with plums, raisins, sausage and syrup – all boiled in milk! And Groningen's brown beans with syrup are famous. Brandy finds its way into specialities, too. *Boerenjongens* is raisins in brandy while in a *Frisian Farmer's coffee* the coffee is laced with lager and brandy. Whilst in Friesland, try *Berenburg*, a spicy liqueur.

Festivals and events Summer: traditional Frisian dances (June–Aug.) in Bolsward. Late June: harvest festival in Bolsward. July/Aug.: tilting the ring in various towns including Workum. Mid-July–early Aug.: Wasschup (a traditional Drenthe peasant wedding) and open air theatre in Borger. Mid-May: Tour of 11 Frisian towns out of Leeuwarden and tourist bike trips from Bolsward.

Bolsward   J8

(pop. 10,000) One of Friesland's oldest towns. Once a member of the Hanseatic League, it is now a busy port and farming centre – indeed, it is home of the National Dairy School. See the **Martinikerk** (1446) which has a beautiful pulpit carved with unusual decorations, lovely vaulting and a celebrated organ the the **Broerekerk** (13th-century) with its superb moulded brick front.

The Renaissance-style **Town Hall** has an impressive tower and beautiful paintings and carvings inside. Nowadays it contains a small museum which holds a summer exhibition. (Open Apr.–Nov.) *Leeuwarden 30km/19mi.*

Borger   K16

(pop. 12,500) A typical Drenthe town, Borger has eleven *hunebedden* (prehistoric graves) in or around it. This is one of the reasons the town has become the permanent site of the *Het Hunnebed in Drenthe* exhibition. The woods encircling Borger are perfect for walkers and cyclists. *Groningen 39km/24mi.*

Franeker   H8

(pop. 13,000) A historic Friesland town that once boasted a fine university (1585–1811) until it was suppressed by Napoleon. A few remnants of its old fortification still stand and the **De Bogt Fan Gune** claims to be Holland's oldest student tavern. Some of the old professors' houses remain like the **Coopmanshuis**, now a museum. The 16th-century **Town Hall** on the Raadzaal with its twin gables, tower and richly decorated interior in stamped leather, is considered one of Friesland's loveliest buildings. On the other side of the canal you will find the curious **Planetarium**, a clockwork model of the stars built by 18th-century woolcomber, Eise Eisinga. *Leeuwarden 17km/10mi.*

Groningen   H15

(pop. 165,000) Capital of the province of Groningen, today this is an important cultural, industrial and educational centre for north-east Holland. Its past has been rich. When it was a Hanseatic trading port, it was prosperous enough to furnish vessels for the Crusades. It was such a desirable prize that it was besieged and captured several times during the wars in the 16th and 17th centuries. Groningen was a recognized seat of learning in 1614 when a university was established here and it is still a lively university city. Note the caps the faculty students wear today are in different colours – a reflection perhaps of the days when it was a colourful arts centre.

You'll find it a cheerful historic city with antique and flea markets, pedestrian-zoned shopping precincts, narrow alleys and impressive buildings. Don't miss climbing to the top of the 15th-century **Martinikerk** which has a 96m/315ft spire topped by a Hemony carillon. The panoramic view of the province view of the province is worth the effort. Inside the church there is a magnificent 15th-century organ and some splendid murals dating from the 16th-century but only rediscovered in 1923 under layers of distemper.

One of the city's features is its numerous *hofjes* – cloister-like almshouses. One worth looking at is **The Peper** or St Geertruidgasthuis at Peperstraat, which dates from 1640. Another is **The Pelster** or Heilige Geestgasthuis at Pelsterstraat (13th-century).

Groningen has six notable museums among which is the **Shipping and Tobacco Museum**, 24 Brugstraat, which traces the history of shipping in the northern provinces and of tobacco in Europe. The **Municipal Museum** on Praediniussingel exhibits porcelains and paintings by Dutch masters and has a whole room devoted to regional costume. If you are an admirer of topiary, look at the gardens in the Prinsenhof where 250 years have produced a masterpiece on the site of an old monastery.

In the vicinity of the city, you will find lots of small friendly villages and a number of stud farms breeding, among others, the black Frisian horses. *Amsterdam 179km/112mi.*

Harlingen   H7

(pop. 16,000) An aperitif to Friesland! Harlingen is your entrance point to the province as you cross the Afsluitdijk. A seaport with a well-preserved historic town centre that includes an attractive **Town Hall** (1730) and **Hannemahuis Museum**. There are boat services from here to and from Vlieland and Terscheilling. *Franeker 9km/5mi.*

Hindeloopen   K7

(pop. 1000) A sleepy small Frisian town on the IJsselmeer, protected on three sides by the sea wall. It was originally built as a hunting lodge for the kings of Friesland in 729 but was given town status in 1255, after which it developed into a wealthy Hanseatic port. There is a Scandinavian 'feel' about the place, with its delightful old houses and bridges and its harbour crammed with small craft.

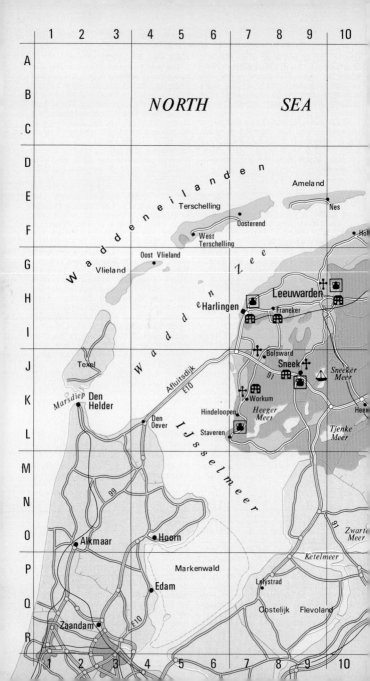

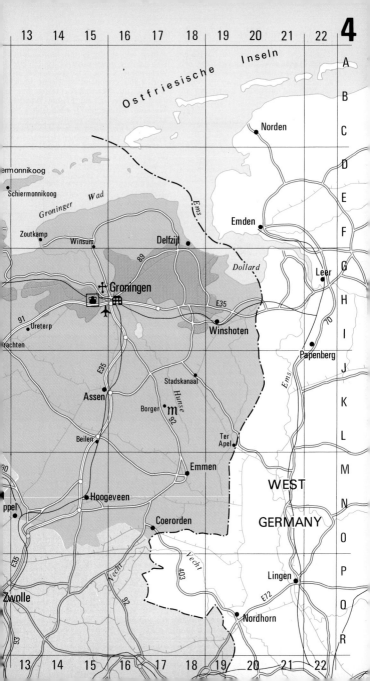

Don't miss having a look in at the **Hidde Nijland Museum** in the former town hall which displays painted skippers' furniture, traditional costumes and interiors. (Open 0900–1200 and 1400–1800 weekdays.)

Leeuwarden   H10

(pop. 85,000) This capital of the province of Friesland is located on a broad highway known as 'The Green Coast Road' which links it with Groningen. This was the first Dutch city to agitate for the Netherlands' recognition of the new United States, which resulted in a Dutch loan of thirty million dollars to America in 1782. And a much later claim to fame; Leeuwarden's most celebrated inhabitant was a lady called Margaretha Geertruide Zelle – a lady whom we know as Mata Hari! A statue of her stands on the Korfmakerspijp.

Situated as it is, in the middle of dairy country, Leeuwarden owes much of its current prosperity to cattle. You can visit Europe's largest indoor cattle market every Friday morning at the modern Friesland hall.

To learn about the history and customs of this part of Holland, drop into the **Frisian Museum** on Koningstraat, Holland's most important regional museum, which houses an extensive collection of Frisian items, including costumes, furniture and porcelain. The **Princessehof** houses a unique collection of ceramics including some Oriental pieces which are the only ones of their kind. The **Natural History Museum** in Herestraat features the flora and fauna of the district.

When you stroll through the inner city, you will see bridges, canals, cellars and interesting old house fronts. Amongst the buildings of historic note are the **Chancery** (1571); the **Weigh House** (1598); and the **Town Hall** (1715) whose council chamber has beautiful baroque panelling. The 15th-century **Grote Kerk** contains tombs of the Frisian Nassau family, ancestors of the Dutch monarchy. Perhaps most impressive of all is the 17th-century leaning **Oldehove tower** the only Dutch tower to possess a lift. Built of brick and stone, 40m/130ft high, it was to have been part of a cathedral which was never built. *Amsterdam 137km/86mi.*

Sneek   J9

(pop. 28,000) An important watersports centre in Friesland's lake district. From the town's small harbour, boats will take you to any of the lakes scattered throughout the province. Regatta Week is held here every third week in August when boats from all over the country participate. Sneek is a particularly popular place for yachting enthusiasts on summer weekends.

Most noteworthy of this pretty town's 17th-century monuments is its red brick **Waterpoort**, whose octagonal towers and narrow arch command the Geeuw Canal. See also the **Martinikerk** which has a wooden belfry, and the **Frisian Maritime Museum**, Kleinzand 12, which has a collection of model ships, paintings, coins and old silver. On warm summer evenings, some of the Frisian women dress in local costume and sing the traditional Frisian songs outside the 17th-century Town Hall.

In between the lakes is some of the Netherlands' best grazing land for those world famous Frisian cattle. The VVV can arrange visits to dairy farms in the area. *Leeuwarden 22km/14mi.*

Workum   K7

(pop. 4500) For centuries, this town in the Friesland lake district, supplied London with eels. Here you can see its 17th-century **Weigh House**, the **Town Hall** dating from 1725 and the 16th-century **Church of St Gertrude** with its detached tower and nine painted guild biers. Belonging to Trade Guilds, each bier has a guild mark. While you're in Workum, look out for the local pottery which is coloured in muted green and brown. *Leeuwarden 41km/26mi.*

Afsluitdijk

The Islands

The four Frisian islands: Schiermonnikoog (**E12**), Ameland (**E10**), Terschelling (**F6**) and Vlieland (**G3**) are holiday resorts in themselves. If you're looking for a peaceful time, they're a good bet, especially since no cars are allowed on Schiermonnikoog and Vlieland. You'll find sandy dunes, woods, bird sanctuaries and beaches plus some interesting architecture. Ferries leave from Lauwersoog, Holwerd and Harlingen.

The islands are family holiday centres, especially Vlieland (pop. 800), an isle blanketed with heaths and woods. Here, the delightful village of Oostvlieland has tiny houses and narrow alleyways, a lighthouse and two museums. There is a choice of hotels, chalets and bungalows and a large camp site. Ornithologists are recommended to come in May or June when the birds nest in the dunes.

OVERIJSSEL GELDERLAND

In only two provinces, Holland shows several faces for there is industrial activity next to farmland and new towns grown out of the ravages of war besides old towns dreaming of a Hanseatic past. There is heathland and rolling hills, fruit orchards and modern housing developments.

The River IJssel gives the province of Overijssel its name – meaning 'beyond the IJssel' and indeed has lent its name to the Zuider Zee, an inland sea enclosed by a dyke in 1932 and only recently renamed IJsselmeer. Here, in the north east part of the province so much land has been reclaimed that the former island, Urk, is no longer separated from the mainland.

Overijssel, situated half way between Rotterdam and Hamburg, combines industry with natural parkland and rural scenery. Roman churches are reminders of its Anglo-Saxon past. Wistful waterfront towns bordering the IJssel River are straight out of the history books. In unique villages like Giethoorn, there is only water traffic and towns such as Deventer, Kampen and Zwolle could tell a story or two, but there are boom centres like Enschede and Hengelo and new tourist resorts in the Overijssel chain of hills like Ommen and Nijverdal, much appreciated by hikers.

Because it is close to Germany, many of the people can speak German. The lowlands of the Rhine stretch into sandy higher country with pinewoods and national parks where game wander – you can watch them from the towers at Ede and Ugdhelegn. This is the Gelderland, filled with memories for anyone who served in Holland during the last war. Few will forget names like Arnhem, Nijmegen and Groesbeek. And it is here in Gelderland that you'll discover the Hoge Veluwe, a large national park with wild landscapes of woods, heaths and sand hills.

Puddings and hotchpotches The people of Overijssel and Gelderland are partial to plain solid good food like the much loved *hotchpotch*, a thick meat and vegetable mixture. Gelders ham and peppered sausage are two other local specialities and the most popular dessert is apple pudding.

Festivals and events Aug. 30: gondola tour of illuminated canals in Giethoorn. Handicraft fairs from April to October in Arnhem. Thursdays in July: street fairs in Kempen. Aug. 20–30: international folk dance festival in Zwolle. Sept. 21: Airborne commemoration in Oosterbeek.

Apeldoorn   J7

(pop. 142,000) Called 'the largest garden city in the Netherlands', Apeldoorn lies 27km/17mi north of Arnhem in Gelderland. In many ways, it is like a vastly overgrown village for there are lots of valleys, forests, meadows and parks between its streets and houses. The **Berg en Bos** is a man-made park although it looks natural. It has a monkey reserve, miniature railway and a lake which is lit up at night. A favourite park with children is **Malkenschoten** and the **Hoge Veluwe** National Park is easily accessible from town. In the middle of the 57sq.km/22sq.mi area of unspoilt lake, forest and moors is the **Kroller-Muller Museum**, a superb collection of Van Gogh paintings.

The Palace of **Het Loo** was built in 1685 by Jacob Roman for William III and his English wife, Mary (daughter of James II of England). Visitors are allowed in the palace park and the royal stables area which houses a permanent exhibition of paintings, prints, furniture, silver and porcelain lent by the Royal Family. State coaches and carriages can be seen in the stable court.

Apeldoorn is a popular summer resort. It has lively cafes, holds outdoor summer concerts and watersports may be enjoyed on its lakes and streams. *Deventer 16km/10mi, Amsterdam 89km/56mi.*

Arnhem   M7

(pop. 129,000) Capital of the province of Gelderland, Arnhem was founded on the site of a Roman settlement. It was a Hanseatic city in the 15th century but as it was held by the French, it did not share in Holland's 15th-century prosperity.

During World War II, it was almost completely destroyed when ten thousand British and Polish paratroopers, dropped here in September 1944 to hold the Rhine bridges for the main allied armies pushing north from Nijmegen, fought against a German armoured column for eight days before 2,400 survivors withdrew. It is this event that makes its name so familiar and it is commemorated by several monuments in the market place and at the Rhine bridge. After the war, the town was completely rebuilt and has been well landscaped to include many parks, playing fields and wooded areas. The parks include: Zijpendaal, Klarenbeek, Angerenstein and Presikhaaf, but the showplace is **Sonsbeek**, site of annual sculpture exhibitions.

Despite so much destruction, the ancient city core still remains, cluttered with tiny antique shops and charming old taverns. In the market square, you can see the 15th-century **Grote Kerk**, the **Town Hall**, the old **Sabelspoort** and **St Walburgiskerk** with its stained glass windows and tapestries. If you make an appointment first, you can visit some of the interesting old wine cellars, open Mon.–Fri. 0900–2200; Sat. 1030–1600.

On the northern edge of town, the **Open Air Museum** at 89 Schelmesweg, has a marvellous collection of original old farm houses, windmills, town houses and costumes etc. (Open Apr.–Oct. Mon.–Sat. 0900–1700; Sun. 1000–1700. In June, July and August, it is open daily until 1930.) Adjacent to it is the **Burgers Zoo** and safari park, Holland's largest zoological gardens,

Open-air museum, Arnhem

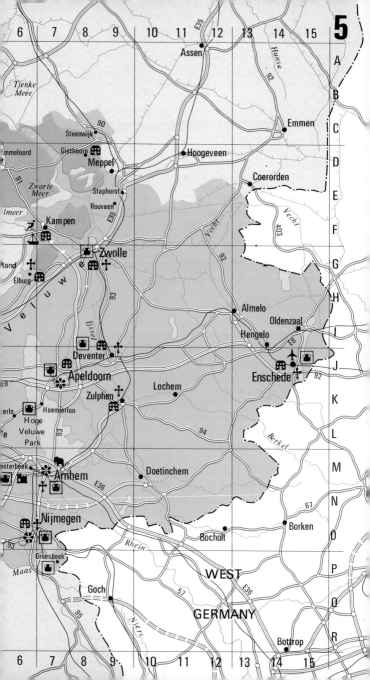

open daily from 0800 to dusk. Don't miss the **Municipal Museum** at 87 Utrechtsweg which has a number of fine 16th and 17th-century paintings, sculptures, furniture and silverware.

Arnhem is a good base for touring central Holland. Boat trips and other excursions are available in town and in the newer section, a wide choice of plush hotels and restaurants. *Eindhoven 36km/22.5mi.*

Deventer   J9

(pop. 65,000) An industrial centre on the IJssel, manufacturing metal goods, smyrna carpets and its own famous spiced gingerbread (*Deventer Koek*). It is an 11th-century town which later became a member of the Hanseatic League. Its historical centre has been restored. Notable buildings include the **Grote Kerk** dating from 1040 with 14th- and 16th-century stained glass. The 14th-century **Mariakerk** on the Brink (market place) was once an arsenal and there are several handsome 17th-century houses on the same square plus the **Muntentoren**, where money was minted.

The Gothic **Weigh House** has an enormous cauldron outside – in 1443 it was used to boil forgers alive! Adjoining the Weigh House is the **Municipal Museum** whose exhibits include an antique kitchen and a collection of old bicycles. Deventer's **Town Hall** contains more than 70,000 16th-century books and manuscripts in its impressive council chamber and there is a picture painted by the artist Gerard Terborch who died in 1681 while serving as the city's burgomaster.

Another museum worth visiting is the unusual **Mechanical Toys Museum** at 9 Noordenbergstraat. (Open Tues.–Sun. 1000–1300 and 1400–1700; closed Mon. and holidays.) *Arnhem 40km/25mi.*

Elburg   G6

(pop. 19,500) An interesting old port and fortified town on the Veluwemeer that is very characteristic of what the country was like before the 'Golden Age'. During the 14th century, Elburg was a rich and important walled Hanseatic town whose 20 gates and towers were protected by a deep moat. You can still see some of those fortifications, such as the 1392 gateway. Of the three town halls, the most interesting is the 15th-century **Abbey of St Agnes** (once an old monastery) which now houses a fine silver collection. The **Oude Radhuis**, home of the 14th-century Dukes of Gelderland, also served as a town hall. **St Nicolaaskerk** (1498) was a castle and the picturesque **Vispoort** (14th-century), overlooking the water, has lots of underground passages.

There are two almshouses worth seeing: the **Weduwenhof** dating from 1650 and the **Feithenhof** (1740). In summer, there are boat trips on the Veluwemeer. *Amsterdam 99km/62mi.*

Enschede   J14

(pop. 145,000) A modern industrial town in Overijssel which is Holland's chief cotton spinning and weaving centre. It has been attractively built, with compact houses and carefully planned city parks and gardens.

See the brick-built **Town Hall**, the theatre, the **St Jacobskerk** and the synagogue in Prinsestraat, reputed to be one of the world's most beautiful. The **State Twente Museum** on Lasondersingel 129, boasts an excellent picture gallery including paintings by such masters as Jan Steen, Holbein, Hals and Rembrandt. (Open weekdays, 1030–1230 and 1400–1700.) The **Textile and Nature Museums** are also worth noting. *Arnhem 88km/55mi.*

Giethoorn   D8

(pop. 2500) A fascinating and quaint water village in Overijssel. There are no roads so there are countless foot bridges and draw bridges and everyone travels by canal. Each house is on its own tiny 'island' and its wooden bridges are only wide enough for one person to pass at a time. Residents take little rowing boats, *punters* or motor boats through the narrow waterways flowing off the main canal. Cows, too, have to be *punted* to their pastures.

Giethoorn is not as unspoiled as it used to be. Tourists flock to the village, to be ferried around in punts, taking photographs. Yet nothing can really spoil Giethoorn's old-world charm. An annual boat procession takes place here on the last Sunday in August. Canal tours take place between April 1 and mid October and last about 45 minutes. On the trip, you will be able to see various farmers' houses dating from the 18th and 19th centuries and the so-called **Vervenershuizen**, homes of the former fen labourers. *Emmeloord 23km/14mi.*

Harderwijk   G6

(pop. 31,500) A popular resort with families, located on the Veluwemeer in Gelderland. It was once a most prosperous centre with an important university on Linnaeustorentje which was closed by Napoleon in 1811.

The **St Catharinakerk** (15th-century) was the university auditorium and is divided by a raised floor. The **Grote Kerk**, partially destroyed when the tower collapsed in 1797, has a Gothic choir. The **Vispoort** was part of the town's medieval defences. The **Veluws Museum** at Donkerstraat 9 is devoted to local history, especially to the rise of the town's fishing industry.

Harderwijk has a small beach and there are plenty of amusements including what is reputed to be the world's largest covered **dolphinarium**. There are several shows a day, with performing dolphins, seals and whales. Boat tours may also be taken on the IJsselmeer. *Kampen 50km/31mi.*

IJsselmeer   C2

The new name for the Zuider Zee which was formed in 1282 when the sea broke through the dunes and flooded the low land behind them. The average depth is 4m/12ft although in some places it may be as deep as 9m/30ft. Over the years, many people had plans to drive back the sea, but reclamation work did not actually begin until 1920. It took twelve years to complete the 30km/18.5mi long, 100m/330ft wide enclosing dam (Afsluitdijk) between Den Oever in North Holland and Zurich in Friesland, which shortened Holland's coastline by 322km/200mi so that the IJsselmeer could

Typical dijk

be pumped dry and give the country ten per cent more soil. The first areas to be reclaimed were the Weiringermeer and the north east polders, followed by South Flevoland and Markerwaard. Work is continuing so that eventually this whole region of Holland will be as it was before 1282 when the Frisian Islands were part of the mainland. Excursions to the Zuider Zee Works can be made every hour from 1000–1700 between Whitsun and September, from Harderwijk. The permanent Zuider Zee Work exhibitions are at Lelystad and Den Oever.

Kampen   F7

(pop. 31,000) This former Hanseatic League city is now a modern industrial port. Tourists are drawn by its attractive yacht harbour and picturesque old quarter. Built in the 12th century as a fortress, by the 14th century Kampen had become im-

portant enough to warrant city gates, some of which you can still see: The **Broederpoort** (now a museum), **Cellebroederspoort** and the **Koornmarktspoort**. Many lovely old houses line streets like the Oudestraat where there is a particularly well preserved house at No. 158. These and the warehouses lining the quays are all reminders of Kampen's rich past during the 'Golden Age'.

See the 16th-century **Town Hall** with its panelled alderman's room and Renaissance fireplace; the new Town Hall next door (formerly the city's wine warehouse); the 17th-century **Nieuwe Toren** for its lovely carillon; and the 14th-century **Bovenkerk** for its fine choir screen. The **Gothischehuis** is also 14th-century.

This is a good centre for watersports, fishing and hunting. *Zwolle 14km/9mi.*

Nijmegen   O7

(pop. 148,000) The largest and oldest of Gelderland's cities, situated on the Waal River. The Romans founded it in AD 69 and built a hilltop fort above the river. By AD 105 it had become a Roman city known as Noviomagus. It was a favourite residence of Charlemagne, who built the **Valkhof** (Falcon's Court) here in 768 for the Frankish Emperors. Only a sixteen-sided chapel remains, but there is a good view from this over the Waal towards Arnhem. You'll have another good view of the city and river from the watch tower by the impressive arched bridge spanning the river.

The **Kam Museum** on Museumstraat has an interesting collection of Roman and Frankish artifacts. (Open Tue.–Sat. 1000–1700; Sun. and holidays, 1300–1700, closed Mon.)

In the Middle Ages, Nijmegen became a free imperial city of the Hanseatic League. During the 16th and 17th centuries, it was passed from Spain to Holland to France before the Dutch finally managed to hold it. See the ornate tomb of Catherine of Bourbon (buried in 1469) in the choir of the brick-built 14th-century **Grote Kerk**, which is located near lively Burchstraat where there are shops and cafes. Also the 16th-century **Town Hall** with its collection of Gobelin tapestries, pictures and furniture is also worth seeing. The **Municipal Museum**, covering local history and culture, is housed in the Commanderie van St Jan (former hospital of the Knights of St John).

Although the city was heavily damaged in World War II, today it is vibrant. Wide and narrow streets meander uphill to join broad tree-lined avenues encircling the old town. Near the city centre is an 81ha/200acre park called **Goffert** which has woods, lake, ornamental gardens and a nature reserve, besides an open-air theatre and stadium.

There are several pretty villages in the vicinity of Nijmegen, including **Groesbeek**, site of a 49ha/120acre open air biblical museum, open daily from Easter to November 1. *Arnhem 17km/10mi.*

Oosterbeek   M6

(pop. 13,500) Adjacent to Arnhem on a hill overlooking the Rhine, this town, once a flourishing Roman settlement, became well known when ten thousand men of the British 1st Airborne Division, under Maj. Gen. Urquhart, supported by a Polish Airborne Brigade, parachuted in on 17 September 1944 to advance on Arnhem to capture the Rhine Bridge. The eight-day battle subsequently fought to hold the bridge against the more powerful German forces has since become a celebrated military saga. Today, Hoize Hartenstein, General Urquhart's headquarters, is the home of the **Airborne Museum**. (Open Mon.–Sat. 1100–1700; Sun. and holidays, 1200–1700.) The Arnhem-Oosterbeek War Cemetery with the graves of 1,745 British and allied soldiers who died in and around Arnhem is near the bus terminal (take a number 1 bus from Arnhem).

To reach Hoize Hartenstein, take the number 6 bus from Arnhem. Also in the area, see **Doorwerth Castle** built on the banks of the Rhine and now the Dutch Hunting Museum. (Open Mon.–Sat. 1000–1700, Sun. and holidays, 1300–1700. Closed Tuesdays.) The Dutch Reform church in Oosterbeek dates from the tenth century. *Arnhem 4km/2.5mi.*

Otterlo/Hoenderloo   K6/K7

There are entrances to the national park, **De Hoge Veluwe**, via both these towns. The park is Holland's biggest nature reserve where you can take biking tours, special cycle routes, signposted walks or roam at will. There are 35km/22mi of sandy hills and woods comprising this park which lies in the triangle formed by Arnhem, Apeldoorn and Ede. It is most famous for the **Kroller-Muller Museum** in the centre, which contains one of the Netherlands' major art collections, particularly of Van Gogh paintings (275 works), as well as works by Seurat, Redon Braque, Picasso, Gris and Mondriaan. Next door to the museum is Europe's largest sculpture park and displays works by Rodin, Poalozzi and

Moore, to name but a few. The museum was given to the nation by a Dutch family. The park itself is open Mon.–Sat. 1000–1700; Sun. and holidays, 1100–1700. Nov.–March it is open from 1300–1700.

While you're in Otterlo, visit the unique tile museum which has tiles dating from 1300 and includes several extremely rare examples. (Open Tues.–Sat. 1000–1200 and 1400–1700; Sun. and holidays, 1400–1600.)

Staphorst-Rouveen   E9

(pop. 9000) Both villages, next to each other, lie just north of Zwolle on the road to Meppel. They boast reed-thatched cottages and farms and are particularly noted for traditional costume and unusual customs. Local farm houses are painted blue, green and white and villagers wear hand-woven costumes. The women wear black or blue floral embroidered skirts with red checked scarves and silver caps with gold side pieces. They don't mind being photographed providing it's not a Sunday when by custom they walk to church in sombre files with downcast eyes, the men on one side, the women on the other. It is best to respect their religion. On a Sunday, motorists and cyclists are stopped outside the village and if you're caught taking a picture, watch out!

The local people have strict morals and rather a strange lifestyle. For instance, trial maternity is general practice. A girl has to become pregnant before she gets married to prove she will be able to keep her husband's farm well supplied with children. No pregnancy – no marriage. On the other hand, those caught committing adultery, are paraded back to back in a farm cart to have abuse etc. hurled at them. *Zwolle 15km/9mi.*

Urk   E4

(pop. 10,000) An old fishing village 14km/9mi south of Emmeloord which for seven centuries was an island in the Zuider Zee. Since 1942, it has been part of the mainland, what is called the North East Polder, but Urk has remained a sea port although no longer isolated. It is noted for its local costumes which are very distinctive. The women wear whalebone-stiffened corsets in a light blue material with chamois leather added to help them wear well, and a broad yoke of flowered silk over it. Often, they wear garnet necklaces, white bonnets and gold ear ornaments which press into the cheeks. The men wear dark costumes, black wooden shoes, black breeches and a black skull cap, all this is sometimes brightened by red and white striped shirts and silver buckles.

Urk is a delightful old port well worth visiting. It has a fish auction, lighthouses and in season, a ferry service to Enkhuizen. There are model ships in all the Urk churches and don't skip the 'Urker' room in the Town Hall. *Kampen 26km/16mi.*

Zutphen K9

(pop. 32,000) An old country town on the River IJssel some 29km/18mi north-east of Arnhem. It has a variety of gables, gateways, old houses and twisting streets plus a world famous church library (from 1561), housed in the Gothic **Grote Kerk** or Church of St Walburg. The church's tower burned down in 1948. In addition to the rare library, it has some good frescoes and a bronze font. See also the 15th-century **Town Hall** on the Gravenhof, the adjoining meat market and the 15th-century brick **Drogenapstoren** gate. Elizabethan poet, Sir Philip Sidney, was mortally wounded in Zutphen on 22 September 1586 while helping the Dutch against the Spanish. *Arnhem 31km/19mi.*

Zwolle G8

(pop. 85,000) Capital of the province of Overijssel, this prosperous old town has ruined defences and landscaped parks. The old moat, the **Stads Gracht**, which made Zwolle a 17th-century stronghold, has become a canal, flowing beneath the former bastions. The remains of the fortifications are the 15th-century **Sassenpoort** near the station.

Other points of interest are: **St Michael's Church** (14th- and 15th-century) and next to it the 17th-century chief watch tower. You can climb to the top of another tower in **Our Lady's Church** (1463) in summer. Locals have nicknamed it 'Peperbus' which means 'pepper pot'. The **Overijssel Museum** is based in a Renaissance-style house on the Melkmarkt to which the costumed villagers of Staphurst often come on a Friday, for the sale of milk and vegetables. Religious writer, Thomas Kempis lived in Zwolle for 70 years and has a museum dedicated to him. *Kampen 14km/mi.*

LIMBURG

Not many people know that Limburg, the southernmost of Holland's provinces, is the second largest market garden region. It is better known for its castles of which it can boast several. Because of its location within a 113km/70mi radius of cities like Brussels, Antwerp, Louvain and Liège, it is popular with families.

Lovers of the outdoor life will enjoy Limburg's quiet north where they can camp in wooded and moorland country or in well-equipped bungalow parks. There are plenty of opportunities for horse riding, fishing, rowing and sailing. There is a historical centre, the major town, Venlo where you can imagine yourself back in the Middle Ages.

The Netherlands' highest hills are in the south of the province along with the castles and the country's oldest city, Maastricht, which also happens to be Limburg's biggest holiday resort. Limburg's chief towns will be familiar to many servicemen. The American cemetery at Margarten, the German cemetery at IJsselsteyn and the many small British ones will recall the fight from Limburg into nearby Germany.

Syrups and mushrooms Limburg's mushrooms turn up as starters or in a variety of main dishes. Syrups are usually a combination like pear and apple. Even the genever is spiced! Limburg's sweet tooth is satisfied with hard cakes, fruit cakes, cakes made with beer, rice, etc; waffles are another favourite.

Festivals and events Mid-May: European motor cyclists' meeting, Maastricht. Summer: handicrafts and folklore festivals.

PEASANT'S HOUSE — OPEN AIR MUSEUM : ARNHEM

Maastricht   O3

(pop. 111,000) The capital of the province
of Limburg and Holland's oldest fortress
town, wedged between Belgium and Germany. There was a community here even
before the Romans chose the site for their
settlement of Trajectum ad Mosam which
commanded a ford across the Maas and
gave this old city its name. There is a walled
labyrinth of underground passages here
and chalk grottoes in St Peter's mountain,
which are 2000 years old. These caves are
about 3km/2mi out of town and extend for
322km/200mi under the fortress of Maastricht and if you knew the way, they would
lead you to Belgium. Inscriptions on the
walls date back to the 13th century along
with autographs by Napoleon, Sir Walter
Scott and Voltaire. During World War II,
the population sheltered here while battles
were fought above them in the hills surrounding the town.

Maastricht might well have become part
of Belgium since it was passed from dukes
to bishops and from Spain to France, but by
1830 it was well defended. Take a look at
the old ramparts along the Maas, especially
the 13th-century **Helpoort** with its towers
and turrets. Altogether, there are 1,450
protected monuments and buildings in the
city.

The **Stokstraat** quarter is particularly
worth seeing. There are many fine churches
like **St Servaaskerk**, a Catholic church in
baroque style. Founded in the 6th century,
it backs on to the main square. Inside, you
can see the gilt and enamelled shrine of **St
Servaas** (12th-century), but the treasury is
the most rewarding with its collection of
religious relics. All of Maastricht's churches have treasuries which may be visited
including the **Onze Lieve Vrouw Church**
built for defence. The Protestant **Janskerk**
(12th-14th century) in the main square has
medieval wall paintings and a 78m/256ft
tower which may be climbed. The 17th-century former Jesuit church on
Bredestraat has been turned into a theatre.

The heart of the town is **Vrijthof**, a
square ringed by hotels, shops and outdoor
cafes. Maastricht is cosy yet cosmopolitan.
In summer, various luxury boat trips can be
made on the Maas and the Albert Canal. The
mountain resort of **Valkenburg** lies
only a few miles to the east.

The American military cemetery in Holland is near Margraten, 9km/6mi east of
Maastricht, on the road to Aachen. *Valkenburg 11km/7mi.*

Sittard   M5

(pop. 44,000) A manufacturing and mining
town but nevertheless a medieval town with
plenty of tourist interest. The best buildings are between the Putstraat and Pardenstraat in the rampart-enclosed town centre.
See the **Parochiekerk** in its quiet square,
which has a 13th-century nave and 15th-century choir with Gothic stalls. **St
Michael's** (17th-century) in the market
has some good wood carving. The **Regional
Museum** in the Old Jesuit seminary specializes in objects from Limburg Province.

Sittard's war cemetery is located at
Ophoven, 2km/1mi away, where there are
250 allied soldiers' graves. 330 more soldiers are buried at **Brunssum**, 11km/7mi
away. *Maastricht 23km/14mi.*

Tegelen   I7

(pop. 19,000) This village is known for the
passion plays held here every five years, the
next being in 1990. These are held in thanks
that no houses were damaged in the last war
and the actors are all local people, so too is
the playwright, and the setting is an open-air theatre. Tegelen is also the centre of the
ceramics industry – there is an interesting
pottery museum in the Town Hall. The **De
Holtmuhoe Castle** is situated near the
town.

Valkenburg   O5

(pop. 17,000) One of the most popular
tourist destinations with many attractions.
Sometimes called 'The Dutch Alps' as it is
an area of 305m/1000ft hills overlooking the
River Geul. It is an old fortified town with
two 14th-century gates and 13th-century
castle remains. Situated at the centre of
pretty valley where hiking, riding, climbing are all possible, Valkenburg's other
features include caves and catacombs,
coalmine, a grotto aquarium plus several
nearby castles. In the summer, it is very
lively place as there is a host of eating
places, hotels, swimming pools, boating
lakes, an open-air theatre and a casino.
Maastricht 14km/9mi.

Venlo   I7

(pop. 62,500) As a frontier town Venlo was
heavily fortified and its architecture is not
typically Dutch. The 16th-century **Town
Hall** has a Renaissance façade and its onion-domed octagonal towers are of different
heights. The **Church of St Martinus** (15th
century) with its 48-bell carillon, was badly
damaged in 1944 but skilfully restored. The
Goltzius Museum at Goltziusstraat 21
illustrates local and regional history and has
fine period rooms and porcelain. *Maastricht
73km/46mi.*

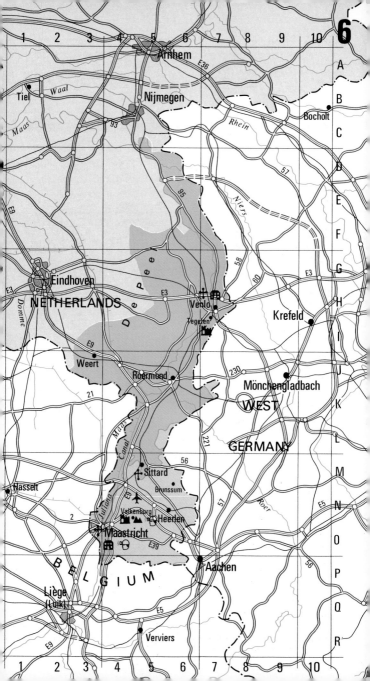

Castle of the Counts of Flanders, Ghent

The Beguinage, Bruges

Torchon lacemaking, Bruges

1914-18 graves, St Symphorien

The Belfry, Bruges

Dampoort, Bruges

La-Roche-en-Ardennes

St Bonifacius Bridge, Bruges

FLANDERS EAST & WEST

You may think that Flanders is nothing but flat country, but this is only true in the west where all the seaside resorts, such as Ostend, are located. Indeed, this coastline is the national playground, bordered by Holland and France, with a 67km/42mi stretch of North Sea shoreline to enjoy. There are broad sandy beaches, lots of entertainment, including casinos, and all kinds of accommodation in the coastal resort towns. Not far away from the golden beaches is one of the favourite medieval towns in all Europe – Bruges (Brugge), the old capital of the province.

When you get to know Flanders, you will realize how changeable its terrain really is: there are many castles and *beguinages* (convents) and a host of carillons. Flanders is a vast garden of flowers. Canals connect numerous towns to the River Scheldt. To the north there are farmlands and orchards. Between East Flanders and the neighbouring province, Brabant, is the Payottenland – the market gardening region often host to fruit fairs and other fairs.

As for the ravaged Flanders Plain of World War I – nowadays many rebuilt and new towns rise in modern splendour from what the British soldier used to call the Wipers (Ypres) Salient.

Waterzooi and almonds The people of Ghent introduced *waterzooi*, a kind of stew often made with chicken although in Blankenberge you can sample it with fish. Seafood of all kinds is naturally popular in the coastal resorts. Try shrimp and gruyère fondue in Blankenberge; *cod en papillotes* (cod fillets with shrimps and mushrooms) in Koksijde; or *paardivisserschelp* (a scallop of shrimps with onions and mushrooms) in Oostuinkerke. Eel dishes galore will be on Nieuwpoort's menus whilst Ostend serves fish and mushrooms in a bechamel sauce. Look, too, for shrimps with a tomato ketchup/sherry sauce in Koksijde which holds an annual gastronomic rally. Belgians have a sweet tooth. Kortrijk pastry is made with egg and marzipan filling. Geraardsbergen's *tarte au maton* is prepared from white cheese and almonds; Ghent's *mokken* are small round cakes made of flour and syrup. Among the other Flanders' treats are waffles (every flavour) and blond butter

caramels in Knokke-Heist; *heksekoeken* (buns made with raisins, crystallized fruit and sometimes filled with cream) in Nieuwpoort; Oudenaarde's St Anne rolls and *lekkies* (tartlets). Two savoury favourites in Ypres are *hennepot*, a cold meat dish of rabbit, chicken or veal, and *taptjesvlees* (calves rib and vegetables). And don't forget the local beers: Oudenaarde has a good one and Kortrijk's is called Diplomat.

Festivals and events Carnival is celebrated with vigour at Aalst the Sunday before Ash Wednesday, at Blankenberge, Brugge – *zottebolderie* (buffoon procession) – and Knokke-Heist. There's a cavalcade at Oostduinkerke the Friday before Shrove Tuesday – *cimateerstoet* at Ostend and on the Saturday, *Ball of the Dead Rat*. The first Sunday in Lent: *Crekelingen* at Geraardsbergen. Third Sunday in May: procession of witches at Nieuwpoort. Ascension Day: procession of the Holy Blood in Brugge. First Sunday in June: *Port fête* on Blankenberge's quays. Trinity Sunday: *Fiertel* procession at Ronse and *Blessing of the Sea* in Blankenberge. Last Sunday in June: *Blessing of the Sea* at Ostend. Summer *cartoonale* at Knokke-Heist and many July festivities in Ghent. *Procession of the Penitents* in Veurne the last Sunday of July. International firework festival in August at Knokke. Every two or three years, *Festival of the Canals* in August in Brugge and every fifth year, the *Procession of The Golden Tree*.

Aalst/Alost   F13

(pop. 80,000) An interesting town on the River Dender. The **Town Hall** on the central marketplace is the oldest of its kind in Belgium. Built as the alderman's house in the 13th century, it was fired by Ghent's inhabitants, but was rebuilt in the 15th century. There is a marvellous view from its belfry which has an image of Charles V in full regalia on its façade. Its carillon is also 15th-century. Another baroque house (1643) is situated on another side of the square and there is also a statue of Thierry Maertans who introduced printing to Belgium. The **Church of St Martin** (15th-century) contains several art works by Rubens. *Brussels 28km/17.5mi.*

Ath   H8

An ancient town, much of which has been rebuilt. The **Tour de Burbant**, the only remains of previous fortifications, has been preserved, ringed by some late Gothic houses. Wenceslass Cobergher designed its 17th-century **Town Hall**. The **Chateau D'Attree**, 6km/4mi southeast of the town is worth seeing for its period furniture and paintings including Watteau. Ath is a good base to tour a number of Flanders' chateaux. *Brussels 50km/31mi.*

Blankenberge   B6

(pop. 14,000) A popular West Flanders seaside resort and second largest on the coast. Its big attraction is the 3km/2mi long broad stretch of beach backed by a wide promenade. On the pier you'll find the **Aquarama**, a show museum with a vast collection of shells, minerals, corals and fish. An informal place, Blankenberge is a summer favourite with plenty of hotels, amusement centres and good cafes in the traffic-free zone behind the promenade.

It offers something for everyone in the way of sports and entertainment with lots of discos, a spacious casino and concert hall. Located from the sea is the old fishing and yacht harbour and adjacent fish market. The **Folklore Museum** is open daily 12 July–15 Sept., except Weds., otherwise at weekends only. The old **Fisherman's Cottage**, Breydelstraat 10, displays porcelains, water colours and small furniture. But there are few historic buildings – the **Town Hall** and the churches of **St Anthony** (1335–58) and **St Roche** (1884–88). You can tour the town centre in a horse-drawn carriage or travel along the sea dyke and pier by miniature train. Blankenberge has two sign-posted walks and a cycle path along the Gentele route. *Brussels 111km/69mi.*

Brugge/Bruges   C7

(pop. 120,000) A dreamy city located near the West Flanders coast which has proved Belgium's most popular destination. Its unrivalled past emphasizes art and culture yet, too, it is a festive little metropolis. Often compared with Venice because of its net-

work of canals and winding streets, it is possibly one of Europe's best preserved medieval cities.

View from the Belfry, Bruges

During the Middle Ages, it was a world market centre for wool and cloth and housed 52 craftsmen's guilds. Its seafaring code, the Maritime Law of Damme, was adopted by all north German towns. In the 15th century, courts were set up here by the Dukes of Burgundy which developed the Brugge School of Painting under the Van Eycks and Memling.

The heart of Brugge is the main square where the 83m/272ft high belfry stands, famous for its 47-bell carillon. There are innumerable cafés around this square where you can sip a coffee and admire the

Market square, Bruges

old buildings. Most of the principal buildings including museums, are within easy walking distance. Many of the restaurants and cafés here were formerly craftsmen's houses. The **Cloth Hall** started in 1248 is here along with mock Gothic buildings of the provincial government. From this marketplace you can walk to Burgplein with its highly decorated **Town Hall**, begun in 1376. The historical paintings by Julian and Albert de Vriendt in its main hall are worth seeing.

In the same square is the **Chapel of the Holy Blood**. The name refers to the few drops of Christ's blood brought back from the Holy Land in 1147 by Dirk of Alsace, Count of Flanders. The Lower Church (12th-century) houses a relic of St Basil. The Upper Church, where the Holy Blood is displayed, was restored in the 15th century. A small museum here contains valuable church antiquities, including silver, gold and gem-studded reliquary made in 1617 by Jan Crabbe, a Brugge goldsmith.

Of the multitude of beautiful religious buildings, see the **Church of Our Lady** begun in 1290; the **Cathedral of St Sauveur**, one of Belgium's earliest brick churches; the **Church of Jerusalem** (1427) and the **Church of St Walburge** (1641), the town's best baroque example. **St John's Hospital** (12th-century) houses the **Memling Museum**. Paintings by the 15th-century Flemish Master, Hans Memling, are on show here, including the *Mystic Marriage of St Catherine*. Also worth seeing is the hospital's old apothecary. The fascintaing 17th- and 18th-century houses lining the long quay and the **Quay of the Mirror** are very reminiscent of Holland. In sum-

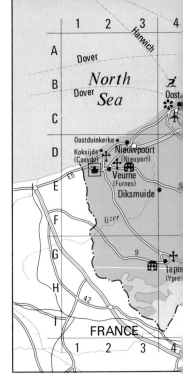

From the Rosehat Quai, Bruges

mer (1 May–30 Sept.) canals and historical buildings are all floodlit.

Brugge, of course, has plenty of museums. The municipal museum houses many Flemish masterpieces. Others include **St Sebastian's Archery Guild**; the **Groeninge Museum** and a **Folklore Museum**. As Brugge is celebrated for its lace, look in at **Seorie House** which tells the history of lacemaking. (Open Apr.–Sept. and by request from Oct.–Mar.) At the Lace Centre, bobbin lace-making is still taught and visits may be made all year round, daily 1400–1800; Sat. 1400–1600.

The beautifully tranquil **Beguinage** (convent) (1245) is particularly attractive. Various events take place through the year in Brugge, best-known of which is the Procession of the Holy Blood on Ascension Day. *Ostend 27km/17mi, Brussels 97km/60mi.*

Damme   C7

(pop. 1000) A delightful little town situated by the side of the Damme Canal and connected to Brugge 7km/4mi away. What used to be a great port is now so peaceful it simulates an old engraving. Fifteenth-century patrician houses can be found on the market square. The statue in front of the striking new **Town Hall** is of Jacob van Maerlant, 'Father of all the medieval Dutch poets' who largely founded the Flemish language. A museum is also dedicated to

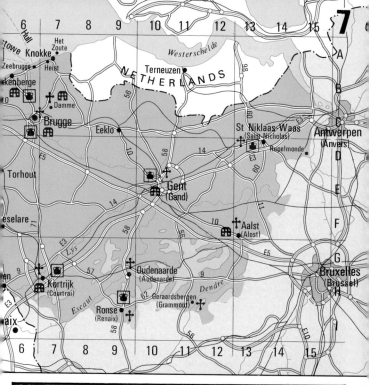

Lacemaking in Bruges

him. Also see the **Church of our Lady** –
climb the tower for a panoramic view. The
Scellemolen, a brick windmill (1867) has
been restored and is open for inspection
Sat., Sun. and holidays. The statue of **Till
Eulenspiegel** by Koos van der Kaaij is in
Damme because writer Charles Coster
claimed his famous character lived here and
was the son of a local charcoal burner. His
mischievous exploits are the theme of the
symphonic poem *Till Eulenspiegel* by
Richard Strauss. In season, regular boat
trips run from Brugge to Damme. *Brussels
102km/63mi.*

Geraardsbergen/ Grammont   H11

(pop. 18,000) An old town situated between
two small hills on the Dender River. At the
restored **Town Hall** is a copy of Brussels'
famous **Manneken Pis**, which was given by
Brussels in return for the original, stolen by
English soldiers in 1745 and later located
here. The modest chateau used to be an
18th-century monastery and the **Collegiate
Church of St Barthelemy** should be seen.
The **Chapel of Oudenberg** is a centre of
pilgrimage, especially on the first Sunday of
Lent with a mixture of Christian and pagan
rites in the Craekelingen Festival when the
burgomaster and alderman drink wine
from a medieval silver cup which has tiny
fish swimming in it. Afterwards thousands
of cracknel cakes are thrown to the crowd.
The town is noted for its cigars. *Brussels
43km/27mi.*

Ghent/Gent/Gand   E10

(pop. 244,000) The former capital of the
Counts of Flanders, situated in East Flanders, and a rival of its sister city, Brugge. It
is a true 'water city' with the Scheldt, Lys
and Lieve all running through it. It is said
to have 200 bridges and 80 islands. It was a
Flemish stronghold, an artistic and industrial centre surrounded by countryside like a
vast garden. No other Belgian city has as
many historic buildings as Ghent, the country's second largest sea port.

For an unparalleled view of the town,
stand on **St Michael's Bridge**. Among the
main sights is the **belfry**, symbol of the
power of the various guilds. The spire is
crowned by a bronze dragon-shaped
weather-vane brought from Constantinople
during the Crusades, and there is a fine
52-bell carillon. Nearby is the 15th-century
Cloth Hall (Lakenhalle) where you can see
an audio-visual presentation of 'Gent and
Charles V', daily except Mon., 0900–1200
and 1330–1700. At the side of the belfry is
St Bavon Cathedral, a mixture of romanesque, Gothic and baroque styles. (Charles V

was baptized here in 1500). Its interior is
particularly rich containing Van Eyck's
world famous masterpiece, *The Adoration of
The Lamb*. There are so many churches in
Ghent that it would be impossible to men-

The Graslei, Ghent

tion them all, but priority could be given to
the **Church of St Nicholas** (1200–1430)
and the **Church of St Michael**.

Old houses abound, especially along the
Graslei. For the best photograph, stand on
the opposite bank when they are reflected
in the water. Another row of ancient houses
is along the **Hoogpoort**. The **Abbey of St
Bavon**, founded in the 7th century is mostly ruins today, but nevertheless, has interesting cellars and a romanesque refec-
tory. (Open daily except Mon. 0900–1230
and 1330–1730.)

The **Castle of the Counts** is enclosed by
the waters of the Lieve Canal. It was built in
the 12th century by Count Philip of Alsace;
John of Gaunt was born here; and the
Emperor Maximilian, Philip le Beau, King
of Castile and the young Charles V lived
here. Its small museum displays instruments of torture.

Ghent's **Town Hall** is oddly designed,
partially flamboyant Gothic and partially
Renaissance. There's a small **Beguinage**
(convent) and countless museums. If there
is only time for one, see the **Museum of
Fine Arts** for its excellent collection of
Flemish primitives. (Open daily except
Mon. 0900–1230 and 1330–1730.) Others
include the **Abbey of Bylooc**, the **Museum
of Archaeology**, the **Museum of Decorative Arts** and the **Folklore Museum** in the
old almshouses of Alyns.

Ghent is beloved by gourmets and hosts
many trade fairs and exhibitions and lots of
festivals. The Festival of Flanders takes
place in August/September when various
international concerts are organized in the
abbeys and cathedrals. Every five years, the

Ghent Floralies is held in the Palace of the Flories. Main shopping streets include Korter, Veldsraat and Bradentdam. Best markets are held in Vrijdagmarkt and in the Kouter. The Prondel market takes place on Fridays and Saturdays in Beverhout Square near St James' Church. *Brussels 55km/34mi.*

Knokke-Heist   A7

(pop. 8300) A West Flanders seaside resort comprising five towns which together are known as the 'Garden of the North Sea Coast'. Five beaches stretch for 12km/7½mi: Heist, Duinbergen, Albertstrand, Knokke and Het Zoute. Between them, the quintet has something for everyone, from family-style to elegant. Sea trips can be made in amphibious craft launched from the beach. The Yacht Club gives beginners' courses and in summer special events are organized for children. The town of Het Zoute may be toured by miniature train in summer, there are signed footpaths for walkers and a well-appointed 18-hole golf course. Knokke is the starting point of the Riante Polderroute ('smiling route'), an attractive stretch of canals and countryside on land reclaimed from the sea.

A good number of exhibitions, festivals and concerts are held here throughout the year. Knokke-Heiste's casino has an international reputation and its health spa has a thalasso-therapy centre. In the extensive nature reserve of Het Zwin, countless nesting birds have made their home. *Ostend 33km/20mi,* Brussels 112km/70mi.

Koksijde/Coxyde   D2

(pop. 8460) An attractive seaside resort comprising St Idesbald, Oostduinkerke and Wulpen. The first is called the 'resort of the flowers' since it is surrounded by four nature reserves. Oostduinkerke has an exceptionally broad, finely sanded beach. From here you can still see the shrimp fishermen going out to sea regularly on horseback.

There is always plenty to do. Sea trips, pedalos for rental, marked bridle paths and cycle routes, to name a few activities. Plenty of fêtes and festivals take place in summer months. There are several museums such as the **Abbey of the Dunes** (1213–1577) which used to be the most important Cistercian abbey in the area, the **National Organ Museum** containing 110 unique mechanical instruments, the **National Fishery Museum** where you can see a typically furnished fisherman's tavern.

Kortrijk/Courtrai   H7

(pop. 77,000) The most southerly town of West Flanders, on the River Leie, and starting point for the *Stijn Streuvelsroute.* Between the Leie and the Scheldt there is an amazing variety of landscape. Kortrijk is a thriving commercial town with good shops, hotels, cafés and annual events. It is also historic. See the market square with its 16th-century **Aldermen's Hall** and 14th-century belfry. The 13th-century **Church of Our Lady** contains a Van Dyck painting, the *Raising of the Cross.* The local Beguinage (convent) is formed by forty little 17th-century houses. The two remaining towers of the ancient town ramparts and castle are the **Broel** towers, and nearby is the **Municipal Museum**. The American World War I **Flanders Field Cemetery** is near Waregem 13km/8mi north on route E3. *Brussels 90km/56mi.*

Nieuwpoort/Nieuport   D2

(pop. 8450) An intriguing small town at the mouth of the River Ijzer. Unfortunately, most of its historic buildings were destroyed in the two World Wars, although some of them were later rebuilt. In 1914, the Belgians opened the sluice gates and flooded the entire Lower Ijzer region, effectively halting the German advance. Among the war memorials is the King Albert monument.

Nieuwpoort has a colourful fishing quay and harbour. The large boats come into port between 0800–0900 and shrimp boats arrive about 1400. One of the town's outstanding features is the enlarged **Euro Yacht Harbour**. Excursions are made in the harbour channel, to sea and along the river in summer. Visit the **Ijzermonding Nature Reserve** created in the estuary of the Ijzer – the only river in Belgium with an outlet to the sea. *Ostend 19km/12mi, Brussels 133km/83mi.*

Oostende/Ostend   C4

(pop. 70,000) 'Queen of the Seaside Resorts', situated in the middle of the West Flanders' coast. The resort's real golden age was in the Edwardian era but recently it has made a dynamic comeback. Wide beaches provide safe bathing and there are plenty of activities and amusements for every age group. It has a world-famous casino and a choice of accommodation. Its top-class Wellington Race Course is another feature, as is the harbour area and fishing quay where you can buy fresh fish at the auction on the quay.

Ostend is a somewhat brash carefree resort and point of Continental arrival or departure, but it has its cultural side as well. There are some museums including the **Fine Arts** with exhibits from different schools of painting; **Museum James Ensor**, that artist's former home; and the **De Plate Musuem of Folklore** which provides historic detail of the folklore of the Ostend area. The former training ship of the Belgian merchant fleet, the three-masted *Mercator*, is now a museum.

The resort has two attractive parks: the **Maria-Hendrika**, 45ha/111acres of woodland enclosing **Koninginnehof** recreational area where there are rowing and fishing ponds, swimming pools and playgrounds. The other, **Leopold Park**, is noted for its floral clock. *Brugge 27km/17mi, Brussels 114km/71mi.*

Oudenaarde/Audenarde   H9

(pop. 27,000) A medieval town in the Lower Scheldt Valley, scene of the battle in 1708 when the armies of Marlborough and Prince Eugene of Savoy defeated Louis XIV and gained control of the Netherlands. See the 16th-century Gothic **Town Hall** which is almost as handsome as that in Brussels and the Romanesque **Cloth Hall**, now a museum of local tapestries. The royal fountain on the same square was a gift from Louis XIV. The **Church of St Walburge**, richly decorated in Gothic style, used to be a Cistercian monastery. Among the old houses, see the birthplace of Margaret of Parma, illegitimate daughter of Charles V. There is an **American war memorial** to the 40,000 Americans who fought in this vicinity in Oct.–Nov. 1918. The dead are buried in **Flanders Field Cemetery** 13km/8mi west near Waregem. *Brussels 60km/37.5mi.*

Ronse Renaix   I9

(pop. 25,000) A town set in the hill country of East Flanders, surrounded by greenery and once the old frontier so the inhabitants are mostly bi-lingual. See the romanesque crypt in the **Church of St Hermes**; the carillon **Chapel of Our Lady of Lorette**; and the ancient **Church of St Martin** with its octagonal tower. The tunnel of **Louis-Marie** was Goering's 1942 hideout. There is a local **Folklore Museum** and on Trinity Sunday, the Fiertel Guilde parade around town. Another celebration called Zotte Maandag (Fool's Monday) takes place on the Monday after Epiphany. These strange processions are tributes to the local patron, St Hermes, who is said to have cured the witless. *Ghent 38km/24mi, Brussels 57km/36mi.*

Sint-Nicklaas/
Saint-Nicholas   G3

(pop. 68,000) In the middle of fruit and vegetable country (Waasland). The market place, **Grote Markt**, in the middle of the town is one of the largest squares in Belgium. The 19th-century, neo-Gothic **Town Hall** has a belfry with a 35-bell carillon, one of Belgium's finest. See also the Renaissance **Chapel of the Franciscan Seminary** with its high altar. The 16th-century **Walburg Castle** is in the town park and features an astronomical clock. The **Folklore Museum** in the Zamanstraat shows curiosities such as an old sleigh in the image of a swan, and also has a Mercator room. Gerard Mercator, geographer, philosopher and

The Harbour, Ostend

mathematician, was born just across the Schedlt at **Rupelmonde**. *Ghent 33km/20mi, Brussels 48km/30mi.*

Veurne/Furnes E2

(pop. 11,300) A small town near West Flanders' coastal resorts, encompassed by pastures. The present **Church of St Walburga** dates from the 13th century and contains a fragment of the True Cross. The relic was a gift from Count Robert II of Flanders who had miraculously survived a shipwreck on returning from the Holy Land in 1099 and gave an offering to the first church he saw (St Walburga's). Veurne's famous **Procession of the Penitents** (last Sunday in July) is said to have its origins in this event. The 16th-century Flemish-Renaissance **Town Hall** is worth seeing for its splendid Spanish leather wall-hangings. *Ostend 26km/16mi, Brussels 134km/84mi.*

Ieper/Ypres G4

(pop. 8900) Anyone who knows anything about World War I will be familiar with Ypres which was destroyed at that time. For four years, it was the most important strategic point on the entire Western Front. It has been rebuilt since that war so it still bears witness to the times when it was a prosperous 13th-century linen town. Successful reconstruction has made a beautiful market square with its two classical monuments – the **Cloth Hall** and **Belfry** plus the **Cathedral of St Martin** (a Diocesan seat from 1559–1802). The Cloth Hall was Belgium's largest; St Martin's, faithfully re-

built, was one of the best Gothic churches in the Lowlands. Two old parish churches which mostly survived war destruction, are **St Peter's**, partly romanesque, and **St James**, which is Gothic. The only old house to survive was the **Templars' house**. Ramparts still encircle the town and the two gates, the **Lille** and the **Menin**, have been reconstructed. The latter was designed by Sir Reginald Blomfield as a memorial to the British soldiers who fell in the Ypres Salient and have no known grave. The Last Post is played here every evening at 2000. In fact, not surprisingly, there are several war memorials and a 1914–18 **War Museum** in the Cloth Hall. The American war memorial is at **Kemmel** 6km/4mi south of Ypres. Some 170 military cemeteries are in the area. Among those best known are Hill 60, Sanctuary Wood, Tyne Cot Cemetery and Polygon Wood. *Ostend 48km/30mi, Brussels 121km/75.5mi.*

Zeebrugge A6

(pop 8380) A fairly quiet seaside resort in West Flanders and Belgium's second largest fishing harbour, most noted for shrimp. The harbour mole extends 2847m/3113yds into the sea. You are free to angle from here or to take to the sea in a sloop, to fish. There are boat trips round the harbour from Mar.–Oct., departing from the fish auction quay. Zeebrugge is associated with the exploits of Sir Roger Keyes who, in 1918, rendered the harbour useless by sinking block ships at its mouth. The **Zeebrugge Museum** recalls both World Wars. *Brugge 15km/9mi, Brussels 110km/70mi.*

The Menin Gate. Ypres

BRABANT AND HAINAUT

Much of Brabant is agricultural. Hainaut, too, has pastoral stretches with some splendid chateaux and parks like Beloeil, but it also has industrial centres, slag heaps and coal mines. It can boast fine cities like Tournai and Mons as witnesses to a splendid past and fun towns like Binche whose carnival is hard to beat. The southwest portion has attractive river valleys and is known as the Entre-Sambre-et-Meuse – with villages renowed for their military processions.

Both provinces are Walloon or French regions (although Brabant is partly Flemish) and it is Brabant which can claim Belgium's lively capital.

Beer and endives Actually, what you think is an endive in a Brussels' restaurant is really a chicory or *chicon*. It is added raw to salads or comes boiled in butter or perhaps stuffed with meat. You can sample it simmered with potatoes and onions, seasoned with nutmeg or garnished with ham and a cheese sauce. Nutmeg is a favourite spice in Belgium – it even gets into the Brussels sprouts! A popular dish in the capital's restaurants is *fricadelles* – roasted meatballs made of minced pork, veal or both. And a good winter entrée is meat in madeira. *Boudins entre ciel et terre* is to be found throughout Brabant but you've got to like blood sausage! Many of the local beers are good: try Diest's sweet dark beer and Leuven's Peeterman.

Festivals and events The Binche carnival on Shrove Tuesday is one of the country's biggest, when the *Gilles* parade. Here, too, on 19 April or closest Sunday, there's the *Procession of St Ursmer*. Third Sunday in May: many military marches in Hainaut like that at Thuin. Trinity Sunday: processions and parades of the *Car d'or* in Mons. First Thursday of July, *Ommegang* comes out in Brussels to celebrate the opening of the Brussels Fair, and on the second Sunday in September, the *Feasts of the Ilot Sacré*.

Beloeil   I8

This splendid castle of the Princes of Ligne and its park have been likened to Versailles. The chateau itself is a modern reproduction, but the furniture, tapestries and Winterhalter portraits are all originals. In the grounds you'll see a small bronze statue of Prince Charles-Joseph de Ligne, who fell in love with Marie Antoinette and fought at the Battle of Fontenoy. The park is one of Belgium's loveliest with a grand lake overlooked by Neptune and his court and several formal gardens. The little brick church is the mausoleum of the Princes de Ligne. *Brussels 62km/38mi.*

Binche   K11

(pop. 11,000) A modest little town only really famous for its carnival. Every Shrove Tuesday, the *Gilles* wear ornate costumes and headgear made of four feet high ostrich feathers, and scatter oranges to the crowd. Binche has a fascinating **Carnival Museum**, with curious and colourful exhibits from all over the world. Only a few of the town's former fortifications remain plus a remnant of the castle of Mary of Hungary, in the public park. The Gothic Church of St

The Gilles, Binche

Ursmer has an interesting rood screen. Five miles north is the Chateau of Mariemont, originally built for Mary of Hungary, sister of Charles V. *Brussels 62km/39mi.*

Brussels/Bruxelles   E13

(pop. 1,016,000) The centre of the European Community gives Belgium's capital its special international atmosphere but its fine ancient buildings, especially those at its heart – Grand' Place – are evidence of the city's medieval power. Brussels' inner town is enclosed by a ringed boulevard. The main boulevards, Adolphe Max, Anspach and Lemonnier cut almost directly through the centre, linking the north station (Gare du Nord) with the south station (Gare du Midi). A striking amount of redevelopment and enormous administrative complexes and commercial areas continually spring up. Brussels is the country's largest city and currently consists of 19 communes.

The bombardment of the Grand' Place by the French troops in 1695 left only the town hall standing. Reconstruction,

Grand' Place, Brussels

Chinese Pavilion, Laeken, Brussels

The Atomium, Heizel, Brussels

The Mannekin Pis, Brussels

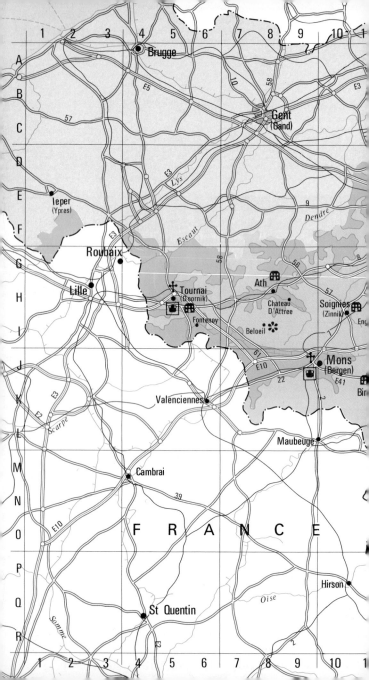

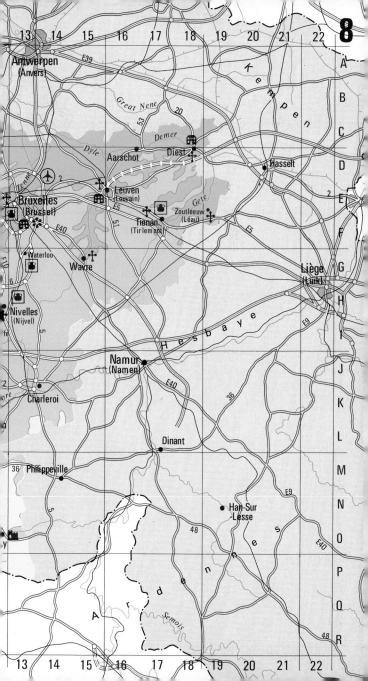

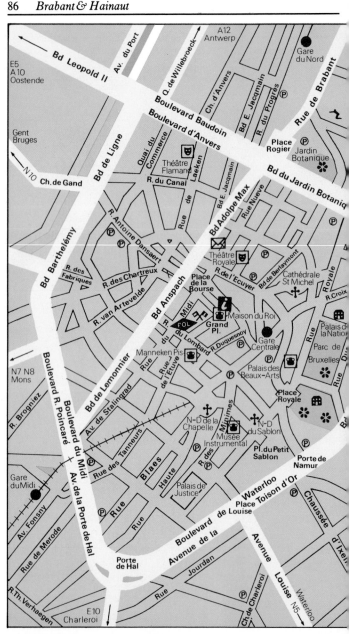

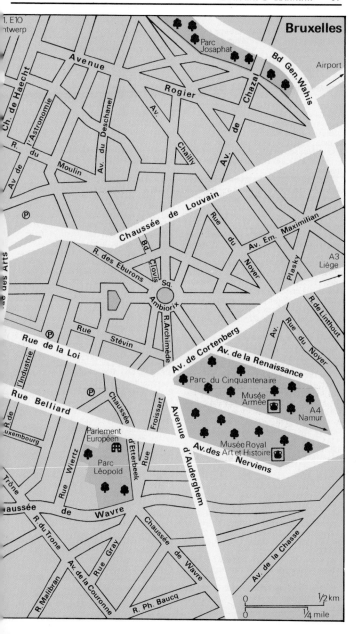

Bruxelles

1, E10
ntwerp

Airport

Parc
Josaphat

Avenue

Rogier

Bd. Gen. Wahis

Chazal

Ch. de Haecht

l'Astronomie

R.

du

Av. de

Moulin

Av. du Deschanel

Chailly

Av.

de

Chaussée de Louvain

Av. Em. Maximilian

Rue
du

Plasky

A3
Liège

Noyer

es Arts

R. des Eburons

Bd.
Clovis

Sq.
Ambiorix

R. Archimède

R. de Linthout

Rue

Stévin

Rue de la Loi

Av. de Cortenberg

Av. de la Renaissance

Av.

Rue
du
Noyer

Parc du Cinquantenaire

Musée
Armée

A4
Namur

Rue Belliard

uxembourg

Chaussée

Froissart

Rue

Avenue
d'Auderghem

Av. des

Nerviens

Musée Royal
Art et Histoire

d'Etterbeek

Parlement
Européen

Parc
Léopold

Rue
Wiertz

Trône

aussée

de

Wavre

R. du Trone

Chaussée

de Wavre

Av. de la Chasse

R.
uxembourg

R. Malibran

Av. de la Couronne

Rue Gray

R. Ph. Baucq

0   ½ km

0   ¼ mile

however, began immediately with the result that today it is one of Europe's most beautiful squares. The buildings are gilded and decorated with ornate architectural touches and embellishments of all kinds.

What to see: Grand' Place is the priority, colourful by day when the flower sellers are here, and equally so at night when it is illuminated. The main building is the 15th-century **Town Hall** whose interior contains many tapestries and ornaments in the successive styles of four centuries. Among the Guild Houses is the **Brewers' House**, now a museum. On the southeast side is the **Dukes' House**, so called because of the busts of the Dukes of Brabant below the pilasters.

On another side is the **Maison du Roi**, formerly the Bread Market. Today it houses the Municipal Museum showing a collection of clothing and uniforms, among other things, for the **Mannekin Pis** located just behind the Town Hall in the Rue de l'Etuve. This bronze statue by Jerome Duquesnoy (1619) symbolizes the irreverent spirit of the city's inhabitants – a famous little statue reputed to be Brussels' oldest citizen, also known as Petit Julien, standing rudely demonstrating his attitude of independence. Every 3 September he wears the uniform of the Welsh Guards to commemorate the capital's liberation by that regiment in 1944. During other months, he wears a variety of costumes.

St Michael's Cathedral is majestically located on top of a hill and reflects all the facets of Brabant Gothic styling. Its 16th-century stained glass windows are superb and the carved wooden pulpit was designed by Henri Verbruggen. Among the many churches in the city worthwhile visiting are **Notre Dame du Sablon**, built by the guilds of archers and other military organizations. Its wooden pulpit (1697) is the work of Marc de Vos. The Church of **Notre Dame de la Chapelle** is another marvellous structure. Painter Pieter Breughel's tomb is in one of the chapels. (He lived nearby at 32 Rue Haute.)

Make sure you visit **Place Royal**, an elegant square built between 1774–80 in Louis XVI style. In its centre is a statue of Godfrey de Bouillon who led the First Crusade and died in Jerusalem. The neo-classic **Church of St Jacques** is here, too. Not far away, Museum Square is the site of the former palace of Charles of Lorraine (1757).

Another lovely square – **Place du Petit Sablon** – was one of the main squares in 16th century Brussels. It is surrounded by Gothic columns on which stand 48 bronze statues representing the city's medieval guilds and in its centre are statues of the Counts of Egmont and Horn.

Of the many parks, probably the best is **Park Royal**, laid out in the second half of the 18th century. To the north stands the **Palais de la Nation** (1779) housing parliamentary buildings, and to the south is the **Royal Palace**, many of whose rooms may be viewed. Among the best museums is the **Museum of Classic Art** in the rue de la Régence, which houses a superb collection of Dutch and Flemish paintings. The **Royal Museum of Art and History** in the Cinquanteniere Park is one of Europe's largest museums with an extremely varied collection of artworks. (Open 0930–1230 and 1330–1700; closed Mondays.) The **Army Museum** exhibits a large collection of military equipment. (Open 0900–1200 and 1330–1600; closed Mondays.) And the **Musical Instrument Museum**, housing over 5000 instruments, is one of the world's biggest. Only 1200 are on show at a time and 50 of these are really special, coming from different countries and eras. (Open Tues., Thurs. and Sat. from 1430–1630; Sun. 1030–1230; Wed., 1700–1900.)

There are two main shopping areas: downtown in the Boulevard Adolphe Max, Rue Neuve, Rue du Marché aux Herbes and Rue de l'Ecuyer; uptown in the Rue de Namur, Chaussée d'Ixelles, Avenue de la Toison d'Or and Avenue Louise. Brussels is famous for its daily flower market in Grand' Place and on Sundays, its bird market. For antiques, visit the Grand' Sablon quarter and if you like flea markets, try the Place du Jeu de Balle, every day from 0900–1300. The Grand' Sablon market is weekends only.

Where to stay: Every category of hotel and boarding house is represented in Brussels. In the top end, you'll find chain names like Sheraton, Hilton, Hyatt and Ramada. A traditional hotel is the Amigo and in a lesser price bracket, the Queen Anne and White Horse, or on a two-star level, the George V or the Mirabeau; one-star hotels are the Continental or the Bosko.

Eating out: There are many kinds of restaurants in the capital. Some of the best located are in an area known as 'Sacred Isle' in the picturesque quarter northeast of Grand' Place. Recommendations in the luxury class include La Couronne and the Maison du Cygne. For tourist class, try Le Marmiton, Chez Jean or the Aux Armes de Bruxelles.

Entertainment: Cinemas, discotheques and cafés are mostly clustered around two main centres – uptown near Porte Louise, Porte de Namur and Avenue de la Toison d'Or; and downtown in the boulevards and streets between Place Rogier and Place de la Bourse. Brussels has ten theatres with plays in Dutch and French. Major concerts are held at the Palais des Beaux Arts. Opera and ballet may be seen at the Theatre Royal de la Monnaie.

Chimay   O12

(pop. 3500) A lively little town bordering with France which used to be one of the 12 peerages of Hainaut. It is the birthplace of Johan Froissart whose statue stands in the pretty market square. He became curate of the church here and died in 1410. The **Collegiate Church of St Peter and Paul** is mostly 16th-century but has a 13th-century choir and a bulbous 18th-century steeple. The **Castle of the Princes of Chimay** on a rocky bluff is open all year from 0900–1200 and 1400–1800. Its greatest treasure is a private gilded theatre decorated with 18th-century cupids and cherubs. The castle was the home of Madame Tallien, an interesting character of the French Revolutionary period who married the Prince of Chimay in 1805 and was celebrated for her soirées.

You can bathe in the **Lac de Virelles** near the Trappist **Monastery of Scourmont** where Emile Verhaeren wrote *Les Moines*. An international music festival is held each June. *Charleroi 50km/31mi, Brussels 103km/64mi.*

Diest   D18

(pop. 20,000) An old fortified town with preserved walls and ramparts. On the market place are elaborate guild houses plus an 18th-century **Town Hall** and the **Church of St Sulpice**. This splendid 15th-century building is richly decorated inside with a frescoed roof and high altar, and houses of tomb of Philippe of Nassau. The former **Beguinage** (convent) (13th-century) features some handsome woodwork and a museum. The baroque **Basilica of Montaigu** (1609–27) is located a few miles from town. Diest has a river beach and open-air theatre. *Brussels 59km/37mi, Antwerp 60km/39mi.*

Enghien   I11

(pop. 9523) A charming town whose 18th-century houses are like those on Grand' Place in Brussels. See the **Church** and the **Convent of the Capucines** (17th century) for their superb woodcarving. The magnificent alabaster tomb of **Guillaume de Croy**, archbishop of Toledo who died at Worms in 1521, is attributed to Jean Mone. Also of note is the **Jesuit College**, the **Church of St Nicholas** and the **Town Hall** which has 16th-century tapestries.

Enghien's chateau no longer exists, but a fragment has been turned into a chapel. The former chateau's park was laid out in the 17th century by the Dukes of Arenberg

on the scale of Versailles. Little remains except avenues lined with chestnut and beech trees, a few ornamental ponds and pavilions. *Brussels 39km/24mi.*

Halle/Hal   F12

A place of pilgrimage as its **Basilica of Notre Dame** contains an unusual statue of the Virgin Mary. Halle's only other claim to fame is that violoncellist Adrian Servais lived here and was often visited by such friends as Liszt.
Brussels 16km/10mi.

Leuven/Louvain   E16

(pop. 86,000) Brabant's oldest and largest university town. In the 12th century, it was the residence of the Dukes of Brabant. Among the university's celebrated students were Erasmus, Thomas More and Casaubon. The buildings were severely damaged in both World Wars but have since been restored. See **St Gertrude's**, **St Peter's** and **St Michael's**, all of which have art treasures, carvings and objects of historic interest.

The **Town Hall** in extravagant Brabantine-Gothic style, survived both wars. Designed by Mathys de Layens and built 1448–63, it is probably Belgium's most lavish civic building. The local **Beguinage** (convent), like a secluded village inside Leuven, has more than 200 17th-century houses on its cobbled streets.

Leuven is Europe's most influential Catholic university. Its Great Hall was formerly the 14th-century Cloth Hall and practically every pretty house in the Naamsestraat is a hall of residence or a lecture hall.

Best of the many monastic houses is the Norbertine **Abbey du Parc** on the edge of town. Its red and grey buildings range from medieval to 18th-century in a lakeside setting. There is some unusual 17th-century plasterwork on the romanesque **Abbey Church**.
Brussels 26km/16mi.

Mons/Bergen   J10

(pop. 97,000) The capital of the industrial province of Hainaut but not without its original character. Previously, it was a city of drapers, brewers, wine and corn merchants. As suggested by its French and Flemish names it stands on a hill and is the administrative capital of the province's Walloon section. Most of the town is contained within boulevards running along the site of fortifications created by Louis XIV after he had taken the town. These days, it is also remembered for the first battle of the

British Expeditionary Force along the Conde Canal on 23–4 Aug. 1914 and the beginning of the historic retreat, and the second battle on 9–11 Nov. 1918 when it was liberated by the Canadian Corps just before the Armistice. Mons was liberated for the second time on 2 Sept. 1944 by units of the American 1st Army.

The small Gothic **Town Hall** on the Grand' Place has an interesting interior. On the left of its main entrance is the 'monkey of the Grand-Garde' – kissing it is supposed to bring you luck. The most dominant church is that of **St Waudru**, a good example of 15th-century Gothic architecture. You'll pass it as you walk up the hill to the ruined castles of the former counts. The

World War monuments, Mons

many treasures of St Waudru evidence the fact the townspeople love art. At the back of the church, the gilded chariot known as 'the golden car' covered with dancing cherubs, is the focal point of the annual procession on Trinity Sunday. Other churches to see are **St Elizabeth** for its Renaissance altars and **St Nicholas** for its 18th-century woodcarving.

The **Centenaire Museum** occupies the 16th-century municipal pawnshop and features coins, ceramics and prehistoric relics. There is also a **War Museum** here, recalling the part played by Mons in the two world wars. The **Museum of the Chanoine Puissant** is in the old lodging house of the 16th-century and the 13th-century chapel of **St Margaret** contains Gothic and Renaissance furniture plus drawings and materials from the 14th to 17th centuries. Local folklore can be studied in the **Jean Lescarts Museum**. All open 1030–1230

and 1400–1800 except Mon. Mons' involvement in the two World Wars is commemorated in memorials throughout the town and there are military cemeteries in Mons, Saint Symphorien and Hautrage.
Brussels 67km/42mi.

Nivelles/Nivjel   M12

(pop. 20,000) A neat little town in the Walloon part of Brabant. Although practically destroyed in the 1940 bombing, it is still attractive and clings to its national heritage. **St Gertrude Collegiate Church** (11th- to 13th-centuries) has been restored to its former romanesque glory. It was the abbey church of a Benedictine Convent founded in the 7th century by St Gertrude then aged 21 when she became abbess. Sadly, her shrine, a 13th-century masterpiece made by goldsmith Nicholas Colard, was destroyed in the war, but the gilded chariot bearing her remains is still annually paraded on the Sunday after St Michael's Day (29 Sept.), and the bronze statuette of Jean de Nivelles which strikes the hours, has been re-installed in one of the turrets. The medieval streets and houses on the church's south side no longer exist, but you can see the **Church of St Nicholas**, containing paintings by Gaspar de Craeyer. The **Archaeological Museum** is in Place St Paul.
Brussels 34km/21mi.

Soignies/Zinnik   H10

(pop. 22,976) An industrial town in Hainaut with many convents. The **Cloth Hall** (15th-century) is worth a look and the **House of Song** on Rue Ferrer is the only one of its kind left in Belgium where generations of singers and musicians came to be trained between 1445 and 1794. Not far away is the **Chateau of Seneffe** (1760) built by Laurent Benoit de Wez, the Brussels-born architect who designed many Belgian monasteries. At Seneffe, the French defeated William of Orange in 1674 and the Austrians 20 years later.
Mons 16km/10mi, Brussels 38km/24mi.

Thuin   L12

(pop. 12,996) A delightful hill town situated on the banks of the River Sambre, split into an upper level and a lower one, each with its own church. That on the upper level dates from 1670 and that in the lower, is partially medieval. An annual pilgrimage in honour of St Roche is one of the military marches in this area. A little way from Thuin are the remains of the **Abbey of Aulne** (656) burned down by the French in 1794. The buildings around the entrance court are 18th-century and are a home for old people, founded by a monk who returned here in 1802. *Brussels 71km/44mi.*

Military procession, Thuin

Tienen/Tirlemont   F17

(pop. 32,500) Called 'The White City' as most of the houses are painted white and have been since they were first painted with white lime to combat last century's cholera epidemic.

See the Gothic **Church of Notre Dame du Lac** (13th-century) which has an elaborate west front and a tower rising to bulbous turrets. The **Church of St Germanus** and the **Beguinage** (convent – one of the oldest in Belgium) are worth viewing, too.

An **Archaeological Museum** is housed in the 1836 Town Hall and on the edge of town, an old church has become a war memorial and mausoleum for the Belgian soldiers who died defending the town in 1914.
Brussels 45km/28mi.

Tournai/Doornik   H5

(pop. 70,000) After Tongeren, this Walloon stronghold is the country's oldest town, founded around AD 50 by the Romans as a strategic centre on the highway from Cologne to the sea. Later, it was home to the Merovingian kings – the great Childeric died here. For centuries, it was part of the French kingdom though later it shared the fortunes of the rest of Belgium. Nevertheless, its loyalties remained French and the Tournaisiens have been nicknamed 'the double French'.

Tournai used to be one of Belgium's best preserved towns with thousands of old houses from the 17th and 18th centuries. Many were destroyed in World War II but restoration work has helped. Today it is a garden town with wide boulevards and statues by Charlier. Despite the bombing, the **Cathedral of Our Lady** (12th-century) was left intact and this plus the municipal treasures, makes Tournai the richest city for art in the Walloon area. This cathedral is one of the country's most remarkable, its most impressive feature being the central group of romanesque towers. The city's medieval sculptors were celebrated and there is a good deal of their work in the church. One striking feature is the black and white marble rood screen (1573) by Cornelis Floris. There are paintings by Rubens and in the sacristy, Arras tapestries of 1402. The matchless treasury contains the silver reliquary of St Eleutherius, Tournai's first bishop, made by the monk Hugo of Oignies. There is also a shrine by Nicholas of Verdun (one of the greatest 13th-century Flemish craftsmen) and a 14th-century ivory Virgin.

Belgium's oldest belfry is next to the cathedral – climb the 260 steps for the view, it's worth the effort. After the war, the authorities limited the erection of new

The Cathedral, Tournai

buildings around the church to one storey so that you can see the cathedral towers, crowned with hat-like cones, from just about all angles. Another survivor was the **Cloth Hall**, gilded in Renaissance style with an arcaded court. It's on the Grand Place. The **Town Hall** (1763) designed as the abbot's house of the Benedictine Abbey of St Martin has been restored.

The massive remains of the 13th-century town walls that held back Edward III, remain on the ring boulevards and the **Henry VIII Tower** dates from the same period. The **Bridge of Holes** (13th-century) is one of the most perfect medieval fortified bridges left in Europe. You'll see some of Europe's oldest houses at numbers 10 and

12 Rue Barre Saint-Brice (1175), and among the most interesting churches are **St Brice**, **St Marie-Madeleine**, **St Jacques**, **St Piat** and **St Nicholas**.

If museums appeal, go to the **Fine Arts** which houses works by old and modern masters, including Roger van der Weyden who hailed from Tournai, Rubens, Van Gogh, etc. The **Museum of History and Archaeology** has countless items, the most notable of which are the famous Tournai porcelains from the 18th century. The Folklore Museum in the **Maison Tournaisienne** shows the town's life and history.

Six miles southeast of town is **Fontenoy**, the battlefield where the British were defeated by the French in 1745. In honour of the Irish Brigade, then fighting with the French, there is a celtic cross on the village green erected by the Irish in 1907. *Ostend 85km/53mi, Brussels 86km/54mi.*

Waterloo   G13

The scene of one of the greatest battles ever – between the British and their allies under Wellington and the French under Napoleon on 18 June 1815. In the village, the small house that was Wellington's headquarters is a museum. He spent the previous night here and wrote the victory communique afterwards. Opposite is the house where Lord Uxbridge had his leg amputated, and the garden in which he built a mausoleum for it. The **Chapelle Royale** (1689) was later enlarged as a British memorial.

The battle of Waterloo itself took place at **Mont St Jean**, 5km/3mi away. Napoleon's headquarters, the **Ferme du Caillou** is also a museum. Do climb the **Lion's Mound** to survey the battlefield, so peaceful now. In a nearby rotunda a circular panorama shows various battle scenes. Arm yourself with *Waterloo*, by David Howarth, the official guide of the Anglo-Belgian Waterloo Committee, if you want to walk over the battlefield, unchanged since 1815. *Brussels 17km/11mi.*

Wavre   G15

A small town in southern Brabant with an 18th-century **Town Hall** which was a monastery. The shrine of **Notre Dame de Basse-Wavre** – in the church of Basse-Wavre – is the object of May pilgrimages. *Brussels 25km/15mi.*

Zoutleeuw/Léau   E19

(pop. 8000) A tiny peaceful Flemish town in the Haspengouw area. In the 13th–14th centuries it was one of Brabant's seven main towns. Stop by the **Church of St Leonard** (1235–1551) for a look at its treasures. The Renaissance style **Town Hall** was based on plans by Mechelen architect R. Keldermans and has some beautiful rooms with decorative fireplaces, but it is only open to the public upon application to the mayor. *Brussels 59km/37mi.*

The market place, Tournai

La Haie Sainte, Waterloo

ANTWERP AND LIMBOURG

To the northwest of Belgium, close to the Dutch borders, much of the provinces of Antwerp and Limburg are encompassed by the Kempen, an area of heather-clad moors and lakes surrounded by fir and pine forests, a region ideal for sports and camping enthusiasts. Because of the number of huge protected areas, you won't find large modern hotels in the Kempen, but facilities for self-caterers are good. The fertile land is due to the care taken by generations of Flemish farmers.

Beauty spots abound, like the central lake, Mol (Zilvermeer) fringed by woods and dunes – or the Kalmthout heath. Landscapes like this inspired great painters like Breughel, while Belgium's second city and one of the world's great ports – Antwerp – is the city of Rubens.

Eels and Asparagus One of Belgium's national dishes – *Anguilles au vert* – originally was Antwerp's local favourite. These 'green eels' are made with sorrel, sage and chevril and, of course, plenty of white wine and you might find them served hot or cold. Fruit grows in abundance throughout Belgium whose inhabitants not only like to eat it fresh, or in tarts and flans, but also mixed with meat. You may well come across Flemish style jugged hare with a side dish of prunes, for example. You will certainly come across Malines large white asparagus.

Festivals and events Third Sun. April: flower parade, Sint-Truiden. Sun. before Ascension Day: pilgrimage, Mechelen – Notre Dame d'Hanswyck. 21 July: processions and festivities, whole country (national holiday). Second Sun. Sept.: fruit and flower parade, Mechelen.

Antwerp/Anvers   C3

(pop. 197,000) A Flemish metropolis and indeed the cradle of Flemish art and culture. It has been a port since Richard I set sail for England after his release by the Emperor. Of course, it is a well-known commercial centre, particularly for diamonds and petro-chemicals, but the tourist will find plenty of historical interest plus tranquil niches. It has always been considered a kind of northern Venice and is the city of Peter Paul Rubens who lived and worked here.

The most fashionable boulevard is the Avenue de Keyserlei where there are cafés and shops. One of the old streets called Meir leads off into the oldest quarter of town. The city hub is the Groen Plaats while Grote Markt is rather reminiscent of Grand' Place in Brussels. There are a number of little cobbled squares around the Lange Nieuwstraat, an area of 18th-century patrician houses and open-air cafés.

What to See: The **Cathedral of our Lady** (1352–1584) is the biggest Gothic church in Belgium, even if only one of the two towers planned was finished. Among its treasures are three religious masterpieces by Rubens, sculpture by Artus Quellin and a pulpit carved by Michael van der Voort. The cathedral also contains the tombs of Isabella of Bourbon (wife of Charles the Bold) and of the famous printer, Christopher Plantin. (Open daily until 1700 on working days.) There are many fine city churches such as the **Church of St Charles Borremeo**, a good example of baroque of Jesuit style (1614–21). Rubens designed its highly original façade and one of its chapels, the **Chapel of the Virgin**. It is rather a sombre church but it sets the right atmosphere for the pedestrian-zoned **Conscienceplein** in which it stands. On Sunday mornings, an antique market is held on this square. The **Church of St James** (15th to 17th-century) contains sculptures and paintings by Rubens, Verbruggen and de Vos. Rubens' tomb is in the chapel here. (Open Easter–31 Oct. daily 1400–1700; 1 Nov.–Easter, 1400–1800; closed Sun. and holidays.) Many paintings by Antwerp Masters can also be found in the rich Gothic **St Paul's Church** open May–Sept. 0900–1200; 1400–1700. Oct.–Apr. 0900–1200. Closed Sun., Mon.

In most cases a small entrance fee is required for the city's excellent museums. Don't miss the **Plantin-Moretus Museum**, Vrijdagmarkt, the printing works of the famous Christopher Plantin (1576) and one of Europe's earliest. His fine Renaissance home is also on the same premises and among the treasures are one of the thirteen remaining examples of Gutenburg's 36-line Bible. (Open 1000–1700). The **Royal Museum of Fine Arts** has over 1000 classical paintings and 500 more recent works. Among those represented are Van Eyck, Rubens, Hals and Breughel. (Open 1000–1700. Closed Mon.) On the Grotemarkt, a lovely quiet square, stands the **Stadhuis** or Town Hall built by Cornelis Floris in 1561–65. Rooms are open for public viewing Mon.–Wed. and Thurs.–Sun., 0900–1500; Tues. 1200–1500; Closed Fri. Opposite you'll see the Brabo fountains (1887).

The **Vleeshuis** or meat hall was built in red brick in 1502. Since 1913 it has contained a museum of archaelogy, history, crafts and objets d'arts. (Open 1000–1700. Closed Mon.) Antwerp's oldest building, the **Steen** (10th-century) was first constructed as a fortress, but is now the **National Marine Museum**. The Council Chamber, still used today, is particularly worthy of note for its model ship collection. (Open daily 1000–1700 except Mon.) Another museum is **Rubens' house** and studio on Rubenstraat. He bought this small property on this site in 1610 and later enlarged it into a little palace.

The port itself is Antwerp's main attraction. Take one of the boat excursions from the landing stage by the Steen (dock 13) for a one or three hours trip. For centuries, Antwerp has been the diamond trade centre. Around the Pelikaanstraat and nearby streets, you can continue to see diamond cutters at work and there is a diamond exhibition at 28–30 Jezusstraat. The **zoo**, next to the central station, is also worth seeing.

On a Sunday morning look in at the bird market (**Voglmarkt**) on the Oude Vaartplaats, which has been taking place since the 16th century. Here you can find old and new goods and even domestic pets. The main general shopping areas are the De Keyserlei, Meystraat, Meir, Huidevettersstraat and the Empire shopping centre.

Where to stay Antwerp has a good variety of hotels in all price brackets. Among the best are the De Keyser, the Theater and the Waldorf. Recommended in a lower price bracket are the Old Tom and the Oud Dijcksterhuis.

Eating out Antwerp can boast many first class restaurants in all parts of the city. Many of the popular kind are located in the vicinity of the Cathedral, in the Suikerrui

Ruben's garden summer house, Antwerp

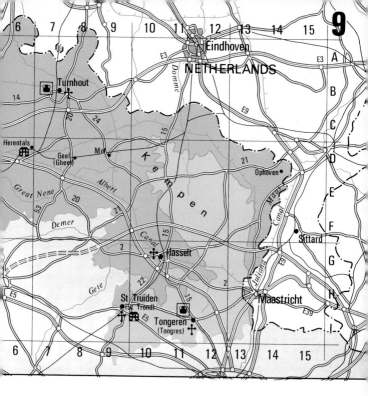

and Handschoenmarkt (glove market). Among those recommended are La Pérouse, La Rade and Sir Anthony van Dijck. A luxury restaurant worth remembering is the Manoir. In a lower price range, try Mosselhuis, Pottenbrug or the Terminal. When possible, look for Antwerp's speciality – which is eels with fresh herbs.
Entertainment Most of the entertainment is to be found in the main square area and in the quarter around the station or the picturesque Schipperskwartier near the Scheldt. Antwerp has its own opera house and is the home of the Flanders Ballet. There are many theatres which feature both local and foreign productions.

Hasselt   G10

(pop. 64,000) Capital of Limburg Province. In the neighbourhood are coal mines and gin distilleries, and it has retained its old ramparts. Its dominant building is the **Church of Notre Dame** which has a magnificent interior. Also see the 17th-century **Town Hall** with its 16th-century carillon;

the **Beguinage** and the **Cathedral of St Quintin**, whose foundations date from the 11th century. *Liège 43km/27mi.*

Herentals   D6

A town on the edge of the Kempen with some remains of its old walls and two gateways. It has a handsome **Town Hall** with belfry and carillon (1400) and there is a monument to the Peasants' War (1522). *Antwerp 32km/20mi, Brussels 39km/24mi.*

Lier/Lierre   D4

(pop. 31,000) The gateway to the Kempen. A delightful little town to walk around with its cobbled streets and a river – the Nete – whose banks are draped with weeping willows. Lier is the birthplace of several famous people including Opsomer, the painter; iron worker, Boeckel; Flemish writer Felix Timmermans and astronomer Louis Zimmer, whose studio is in an old tower on Zimmerplein 18 with an astronomical clock which he completed in 1930 – the *Centenary Clock.* (Open summer 0900–

1200 and 1300–1900; winter 0900–1200 and 1400–1600.)

The 18th-century **Town Hall**, situated on the Grotemarkt, has a magnificent winding staircase and ornate interior. Next to it is the belfry (1369) in which every evening the last municipal watchman closets himself until dawn, sounding a trumpet at hourly intervals. Among the churches is **St Gommarus** whose beautifully carved rood screen is so delicate it resembles lace. *Antwerp 17km/11mi.*

Mechelin/Malines   F4

(pop. 78,000) For centuries *the* religious centre of Belgium and the seat of the country's only archbishop, so not surprisingly it is a town full of churches, colleges and convents. It is also world renowned for its carillon bells. Most of the bell ringers you'll hear elsewhere will have been trained in Mechelen.

See the **Cathedral of St Rombout**, begun in the 13th century. Its finest point is its 97m/318ft tower containing a 49-bell carillon which strikes briefly every quarter of an hour. On some summer evenings, the town carilloneur gives recitals here. Inside the church are black and white marble altars and exquisite fittings; beautiful stained-glass windows and paintings by Van Dyck among others. The baroque high altar was designed by Luc Fayd'herbe (1617–97), chief craftsman of the Mechelen family of six sculptors, two of whom were women. He also designed the **Church of Notre Dame d'Hanswijk**. Another Mechelen native was Theodore Verhaegen (1700–89), perhaps best of all 18th-century Belgian sculptors. Designs and paintings by Rubens like the *Adoration of the Magi* in the **Church of St John** can be found in Mechelen.

The hub of the town is the **Grotemarkt**, dominated by the Town Hall, formerly the Cloth Hall, a strange building erected over 300 years. The Gothic official house of the mayor **Schepenhuis**, (1374) was once a town hall but now holds the city's archives. Mechelen has many quaint, interesting houses. One, originally the home of humanist De Busleyden (1507) is now the **Municipal Museum** (Stadsmuseum) which represents local history and has a special section devoted to the carillon. (Open Easter–Sept. 1000–1200 and 1400–1700.) Notable houses are the **House of the Salmon** – the 16th-century fishermen's guild house – and the **House of the Devil**.

Artistic and historic, Mechelen is additionally a market town, famous for its asparagus. Buy the local beer called Gouden Carolus and look at its tapestry and lacework. Tapestry-making has been a tra-ditional craft here for a long time and two weaving shops are still active. *Antwerp 23km/14mi, Brussels 24km/15mi.*

Sint Truiden/St Trond   H9

(pop. 36,000) A pleasant town in the middle of fruit orchard – Haspengouw – country. There is a colourful fruit market in **Grotemarkt** on the centre of which stands the 18th-century Town Hall with its brick 17th-century belfry. Nearby are the ruins of an old Benedictine Abbey. See the ancient churches of **St Peter** and **St Gangulphe**, fine romanesque examples. The **Beguinage** (convent) houses date from the 17th and 18th century and in their church are several interesting murals. Opposite the church is the astronomical clock by K. Festraets which has more than 20,000 parts. At each hour, death appears with twelve medieval craftsmen. *Liège 35km/22mi, Brussels 64km/40mi.*

Tongeren/Tongres   I12

(pop. 30,000) One of Belgium's oldest towns founded in the first century AD with many visible relics from its Roman and Frankish past. You can see the remains of the medieval ramparts near the **Vise Gate** and outside them those of a Roman wall. In the **Provincial Gallo-Roman Museum**, there are over 18,000 items dating from pre-historic times. (Open daily 0900–1200 and 1400–1700. Closed Mon.) The Grotemarkt is the bustling town centre, site of the 18th-century Town Hall and dominated by the **Basilica of Notre-Dame**. The latter has a charming little romanesque cloiser and an extremely rich treasury containing among other things, the red tunic and gold with ivory cross of St Gervais who became Bishop of Tongeren in AD 346. The greatest treasure, though, is perhaps the reliquary of the Holy Martyrs of Trier, an 11th-century work. June concerts are held in the Basilica which is open Mon.–Sat. 0900–1200 and 1400–1830; Sun. and holidays 1400–1830. The **Treasury** is open May 1–30 Sept. 0900–1200 and 1400–1700. *Liège 19km/12mi, Brussels 83km/52mi.*

Turnhout   B7

(pop. 37,000) A small town in the Kempen where playing cards and prayer books are manufactured. Its Law Courts used to be the castle of the Dukes of Brabant; the old **Beguinage** (convent); the **Church of St Peter** which has several remarkable carved oak pulpits; the **Taxandira Museum** with its items relating to Kempen folklore; the unusual **Museum of Playing Cards**. *Antwerp 41km/25.5mi.*

THE ARDENNES
NAMUR LIÉGE LUXEMBOURG

The beautiful forested high plateau of the Ardennes encompasses much of the three provinces of Liège, Luxembourg and Namur. It is a region of castles, abbeys, flowers, woods and rivers and is perhaps at its best in the spring. It is an area of small hotels and wayside inns, not to mention the local specialities such as the hams, pâtés, woodcock and venison. There are good camping and caravan sites and lots of sporting possibilities. The streams and rivers are all well stocked and there are boating and bathing facilities.

Highest part of the Ardennes is called the High Fagnes (fens) at an altitude of more than 610m/2000ft above sea level. It begins just beyond Spa and reaches up to Baraque Michel 675m/2123ft. From December to March, this area can be excellent for skiing with snow conditions equal to those in many higher European resorts. Beauty spots are abundant in this high plateau lying in the basins of the Rhine, Mosel and Meuse; like Tilff, a favourite weekend resort in the Ourthe Valley, 11km/7mi south of Liège – or St Hubert, a delightful town in the Forest of St Hubert. You will discover lakes galore, like the Talsperre or Eupener See at Eupen, Belgium's largest, and there are also grottoes and caves. The marvellous caves at Dinant appear to be the work of the little people and at Remouchamps there is the longest subterranean river. The Ardennes, too, is where you will find health resorts like Spa, patronized for many years by royalty.

Goose and flamiche Goose is served in a variety of ways in the Ardennes where each town has its own methods of cooking. One of the best is Visé where it is prepared with wine and cream having first been cooked in bouillon and lightly fried. Goose pâté is a popular Namur starter while beef with beer comes next and in Liège you're likely to find veal kidneys in cognac. All Ardennes food is cooked with style – try *escaveche de la Meuse* (river trout and cray fish) in Dinant, a town whose flamiches (cheese tarts) are famous. Tarts of all kinds are regional specialities such as *tarte au riz* (rice tart) and a *gozette* (apple turnover) served in Visé.

Festivals and events Four days before Lent: carnival, Malmédy. Mon. before Ash Wednesday: *Rosenmontag* procession, Eupen. Mid-Lent: processions, Hasselt and Stavelot with *blancs moussis* at Stavelot. Sun. following St George's Day: archery competition, Visé. June: shooting tournaments throughout Limburg. Aug. 15: floral parade and battle of flowers, Spa.

Andenne   F10

(pop. 8000) An ancient Carolingian city on the right bank of the Meuse between Namur and Huy. It grew up around a religious community founded by St Begge (whose tomb is in the 18th-century church here). She was the mother of Pepin de Herstal and the grandmother of Charles Martel. The powerful Pepin family included the great Charlemagne. Andenne became a centre of craftsmen and even today produces unusual pottery. A collection of regional stone work, clay pipes and pottery may be seen in the **Museum of Ceramics** housed in the Town Hall. (Open May–Sept., Tues.–Sun. 1430–1730.) *Namur 21km/13mi, Brussels 75km/47mi.*

Anseremme   I8

Once an artists' haven on the Meuse, near the mouth of the Lesse valley. See the little church and priory remains (largely 17th century) on a small peninsula of meadowland. The cliffs along the river here are oddly shaped creating such rock formations as the Gully of Colebi and the Caverns of Furfooz. Below Anseremme is the **Chateau de Freyr** whose gardens are said to have been designed by Le Nôtre, based on those at Versailles with fountains, orange trees and a maze. Coffee was served for the first time in Belgium at this chateau when Louis

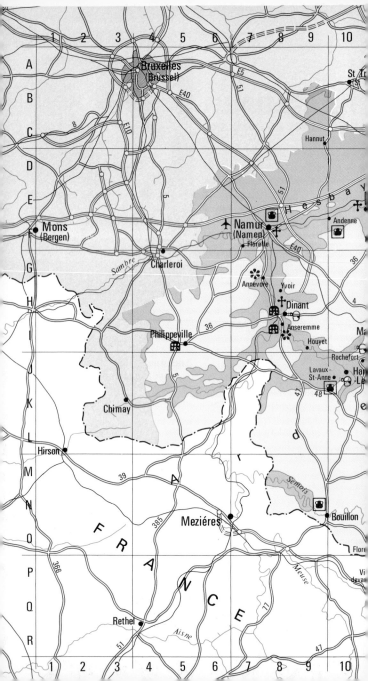

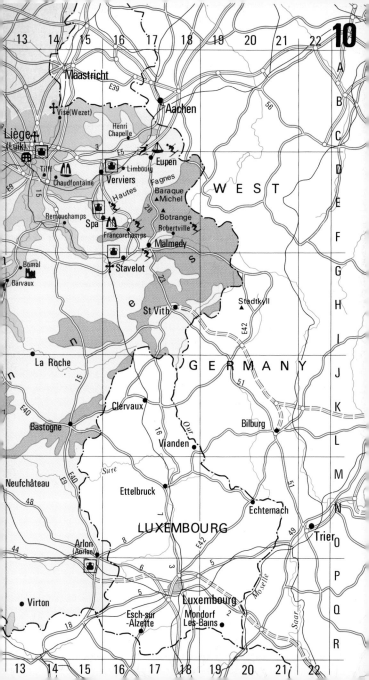

XIV of France and Charles II of Spain signed a treaty (1675). *Dinant 4km/2.5mi, Brussels 95km/59mi.*

Arlon/Aarlen   O15

(pop. 23,000) The capital of the province of Luxembourg, located near the source of the Semois. It was from here that Richard the Lion Heart left for the Crusades. Arlon was burned by the Duke of Guise in 1558, re-fortified by Vauban in the 17th century. Many Roman remains from the area can be seen in the **Archaeological Museum**. *Brussels 191km/119mi.*

Bastogne   L15

(pop. 7000) This town situated on the edge of the Ardennes is best remembered for its part in the 1944 Ardennes Offensive when 19,000 American soldiers died in one week. The American resistance and ultimate victory are commemorated by several monuments, the most impressive of which is the Mardasson consecrated to this 'Battle of the Bulge'. Next to it is the **Historical Centre**, telling the story of the battle, open daily 0800–1700 June–Aug.; March, Apr., May and Sept. 0900–1800; Oct.–15 Nov. 1000–1700. A Sherman tank stands in the main square as a perpetual reminder and the milestones and gun turrets along the roads mark the advance of the liberating armies.

Bastogne was an important market town in the 7th century and by the 17th century had been dubbed 'The Paris of the Ardennes'. *Namur 91km/57mi, Brussels 152km/95mi.*

Bouillon   N9

(pop. 3000) The largest tourist centre in the Semois valley in a lovely wooded setting. This is the birthplace of Godfrey de Bouillon and at one time was capital of a small duchy of the same name. De Bouillon sold the duchy to the Bishops of Liège to raise money for the First Crusade in which he died in Jerusalem. You can visit the fortified, medieval **castle**; the **Museum of Godfrey of Bouillon** with souvenirs of the Crusades; and the **Ducal Museum** where local crafts are displayed in an 18th-century town house. Open daily July–Aug. 0900–1900; Apr., May, June and Sept. 0900–1800; March, Oct., Nov. 0900–1700; Jan., Feb., Dec. 0900–1700 except Mon. and Tues., if weather allows. *Liège 119km/75mi, Brussels 161km/101mi.*

Chaudfontaine   D14

(pop. 3000) A small spa in the valley of the Vesdre with the only hot mineral springs in

Belgium. A great place for relaxing, surrounded by wooded hills and close to a number of castles. The thermal institute treats rheumatism and gout. *Liège 9km/5.5mi.*

Dinant   H8

(pop. 12,000) A popular tourist centre on the Meuse which before World War I was a perfect medieval town. It is said to have suffered over 600 civilian deaths in World War I and 1100 houses were destroyed. In the second war it was bombarded and partly burnt out. Its **Collegiate Church of Notre Dame** is good early Gothic with a pear-shaped bell tower, set against the lofty citadel which is perched on a crag 100m/328ft above the Meuse. Both the citadel and its museum may be reached by chair lift. A chair lift also operates to the **Montfort Tower** for a superb panoramic view. Dinant was the birthplace of Adolphe Sax (1814–94), inventor of the saxophone, whose house is now a museum.

As Dinant is the main tourist centre in

Dinant

the Ardennes there are all kinds of sport and entertainment facilities including fantastic prehistoric caves, miniature golf, tennis, fishing, boating and a casino. The caves of Dinant are known as **La Merveilleuse**, their best feature being the fine white stalactites; shops are filled with the copper ware or *Dinanderie* for which Dinant was celebrated as long ago as the 12th century. *Namur 28km/17.5mi, Brussels 106km/66mi.*

Durbuy   G12

(pop. 300) Belgium's smallest town located on the Ourthe River, and a good holiday centre. It was first privileged with the title of 'town' in 1331. An old bridge spans the river and nearby is the castle of the Counts of Ursel, restored in 1880. In the main street of Durbuy is a fine half-timbered house (16th-century) called 'Spanish House' or Corn Exchange. Fishing and hunting enthusiasts will appreciate the wooded valleys of the Ourthe and the Aisne. Two miles from Durbuy is **Barvaux-sur-Ourthe** where you see prehistoric dolmen and standing stones. At Bomal-sur-Ourthe, 5km/3mi, you will find the **Castle of Logne** plus some ancient Frankish cemeteries. *Liège 51km/31mi, Brussels 119km/74mi.*

Eupen   D17

(pop. 17,000) On the edge of the Hertogenwald Forest near the German frontier, this town is in the German-speaking part of Belgium. It was one of three cantons transferred from Germany to Belgium after the First World War. It is a good holiday

Rosenmontag, Eupen

centre largely due to its dam which gives Belgium its largest artificial lake. There's a beach here and yachting, canoeing and other watersports may be practised. The small narrow-streeted town has a few old patrician 18th-century houses and St Nicholas Church. Much of the surrounding countryside is part of the Belgo-German Nature Reserve. The American military cemetery of **Henri Chapelle**, 7km/4mi away, has 8,000 graves, a chapel and memorial museum. *Liège 40km/25mi.*

Floreffe   F7

A little place best known for its grottoes, the only caves in Belgium of calcareous and dolomitic structure with magnificent chambers and rock formations in spectacular colours. Its old abbey (today a seminary) spans five centuries of architecture and is the dominant building in town, indeed in the Valley of the Sambre. The military march of St Peter takes place here on the first Sunday after 29 June with old military costumes and arms. *Brussels 71km/44mi.*

Florenville   O11

(pop. 2600) A holiday centre set above the Semois River. It was founded in the 12th century and in 1793 it was the centre of a peasant revolt against the French. Florenville is a good base for exploring the encompassing countryside and boasts numerous accommodations. Excursions can be made from here by boat to **Lacuisine** and **Chiny** with its ruined castle. Another side trip could take you to Villers-devant-Orval near the French frontier, where there is the Trappist Abbey of Orval. The new abbey stands alongside the romanesque and Gothic ruins of the medieval abbey while the abbey's brewery and dairy are widely recognized for their beer and cheese. *Brussels 177km/110mi.*

Francorchamps   F16

(pop. 1000) A sports centre high in the Fagne Hills where there is a bob sleigh run, a national motor racing circuit and shooting contests. The Botanical Tree Garden is worth seeing and the national park of the Upper Ardennes easily accessible. *Liège 44km/27mi, Brussels 142km/90mi.*

Han-sur-Lesse   J10

(pop. 700) A village on the fringes of the Ardennes, entry point to the Grottoes of Han, possibly the most beautiful and largest subterranean network in Europe. A visit here (close to two hours) will take you into another world - of stalagmites, stalactites, galleries, domes and gigantic chambers which have fanciful names like 'The Tiara' or 'The Alhambra'.

In the vicinity of Han there's a wild animal reserve closed only in Jan. and Feb. Sixteen years of findings about the waters of the subterranean River Lesse have been correlated to form the Museum of the Subterranean World, closed only in Jan. and Feb. The chateau of **Lavaux-St-Anne**, a fortified feudal manor house containing the national Hunting Museum, is located 9km/5mi away. *Namur 59km/37mi, Brussels 119km/74mi.*

Huy   E11

(pop. 18,000) A town of the Meuse famous
for its pewter wares. It received one of the
first parish charters in all Europe in 1066
and later became a centre for craftsmen
specializing in gold and enamel work. Today, there are papermills, tanneries and
foundries alongside artisans' workshops.

Use the cable car to get to the top of the
massive Dutch-built citadel (1818) for an
unparalleled view of the town and Meuse
Valley. From this vantage point you can see
the old multi-arched 13th-century bridge
spanning the river (restored many times)
and the **Collegiate Church of Notre Dame**
with its highly decorated tower front. In the
market place is a much admired copper
fountain (early 15th-century) and the
Town Hall in Louis XV style. You'll find
the flower market on this square and cafés
where you can sample the local cheese and
wine.

There are several old churches and convents to see. Amongst the notable, **St Peter's** has 12th-century baptismal fonts and
the old monastery of the Franciscans, with
its attractive cloister, is now the **Folk
Museum**. The Hotel de la Cloche and the
Maison du Ponton are both handsome old
houses. In the ruined Abbey of Neufmous-
tier on the eastern side of town is the tomb
of Peter the Hermit whose preaching led to
the First Crusade, and who died here in
1115.

To the south of Huy you'll find the
chateau of **Modave**, a feudal castle with
Renaissance additions. The Order of the
Garter was conferred on the owner by
Charles II while he was in exile in Bruges.
Huy is a romantic little town which caters
for most sports. *Liège 33km/20mi, Brussels
83km/52mi.*

La Roche-en-Ardenne   J13

(pop. 4000) A highly favoured beauty spot
and holiday centre in the Ourth Valley
noted for its local pottery, Ardennes cooking and as a base for scenic walks. The town
and river valley are overlooked by the
ruined castle of the Counts of La Roche
where a *son et lumière* show is presented in
summer. A game and forest park are close
by, and may be reached by a special tourist
train. Rowing boats, kayaks and pedalos
are available for hire on Lake La Roche in
season. *Liège 71km/44mi, Brussels 129km/
80mi.*

La-Roche-en-Ardenne

Liège/Luik   C13

(pop. 224,000) An industrial city and the
French-speaking capital of Wallonia. It is
the gateway to the Ardennes and has always
been rather an independent city after a long
succession of prince-bishops gave it pri-
vileges and immunity from the ruling reg-
imes of Burgundy, Spain and Austria. The
inhabitants, however, are recognized for
their good nature by the Punch-figure,
Tchantches. During the Middle Ages, Liège
was a craft centre which specialized in
brasswork and iron work, creating fine
swords and small firearms. Only later on
did it develop into an industrial town.

Despite the foundries located here today,
Liège is a handsome city with well laid-out
boulevards and gardens with a hub around
St Lambert Square and Market Square.
Seventeenth and 18th-century buildings
border Market Square — the **Town Hall** is
marked by its double-headed Habsburg
eagle. The lovely fountain (1698) in the
square's centre is known as **The Perron,** in
the past the symbol of freedom of the
citizens of Liège, and now the symbol of the
city.

Liège claims many great churches. The
Cathedral of St Paul, founded in 971, but
for the most part Gothic, has an exquisite
interior and in its treasury, the shrine of St
Lambert, a reliquary bust in gilded silver
(1512) plus a group of figures including
Charles the Bold and St George crafted in
gold (1471). Architecturally, the **Church of
St James** is probably more interesting as it
is in several different styles. Most of it is
flamboyant Gothic — the north portal is a
little masterpiece while the choir has five
immense Renaissance stained-glass windows.

The romanesque **Church of St Barth-
olomew,** on Place Saint-Barthélémy, is
most famous for the bronze baptismal font,
made by Renier of Huy around 1112, which
is the finest specimen of romanesque carving in Belgium. Other notable churches
include the **Church of St John,** the **Church
of The Holy Cross** and the **Church of St
Denis.**

You'll need time to tour all of Liège's
museums. The **Curtius Museum,** with displays of applied arts and antiquities, is
located in an early 17th-century mansion.
In the same building, the **Glass Museum**
exhibits magnificent Phoenician and Belgian glassware. Open 1000–1230 and 1400–
1700, Sun. 1000–1600. Closed Tues.
Ansembourg Museum, in a 1735 patrician
house, is devoted to the decorative arts and
18th-century Liège furniture. Modern
paintings are displayed at the **Museum of
Fine Arts** and the **Gretry Museum** contains several souvenirs and articles relating
to the Belgian composer. Don't miss the

Museum of Walloon Life (in a 17th-
century convent). It concentrates on Walloon crafts and arts with a first class puppet
collection, dominated by the *Tchantches* –
incarnation of the good nature and jollity of
Liège citizens. In winter, the local puppet
theatres put on regular shows.

The most popular quarter of Liège is the
Outremeuse area. A multitude of items are
for sale at the Batte, the Sunday morning
market held on the left bank of the Meuse
on the Quai de la Batte, from 0800–1400. In
the shops look for traditional Liège pro-
ducts such as hunting rifles, usually finely
engraved, or Val-Saint-Lambert crystal.
The city houses the Walloon Opera and also
has several theatres besides the puppet
theatre. The main shopping streets include
the Boulevards D'Avroy and de la Sauvenière and cathedral district. *Brussels 98km/
62mi, Ostend 222km/140mi.*

Malmédy   F17

(pop. 7000) A carnival town which was well
reconstructed after being ravaged by the
Ardennes Offensive in 1944–5. It was one
of the three districts recovered from Germany in 1918 and the German influence is
still very strong, quite visible in the slate
hung older houses. The 18th-century
Abbey Church escaped the destruction and
the Abbey chapter house is now a small
museum illustrating local history and folklore. You can stay in the holiday resort of
Robertville, 9km/5mi to the north-east, on
the edge of a lake at the foot of the Upper
Fagne National Park where there are several good hotels and restaurants. *Liège 60km/
37.5mi, Brussels 152km/95mi.*

Namur   F8

(pop. 101,000) Gateway to the Ardennes,
this city is situated on the Meuse near its
junction with the Sambre. Because of its
strategic position, Namur has been the
stage for many battles yet today is a serene
town, one of Belgium's most attractive. It is
dominated by the citadel, accessible by
winding road or by cable car. Taken from
the French by the British in 1695, it houses
a weapons and forestry museum today.

The **Cathedral of St Aubain,** on the
Place St Aubain, was rebuilt in the 18th
century by Pizzoni. Behind its high altar is a
little black marble cenotaph containing the
heart of Don John of Austria, Philip II's
brother, brilliant victor of Granada and
Lepanto who died mysteriously at Namur
in 1578. Opposite, the former bishop's
palace (18th-century) is now the seat of the
provincial government. The **Diocesan
Museum** adjoins the Cathedral and among
its treasures are the jewel-studded gold
crown given by Baudouin, Emperor of

Constantinople in the 13th century plus many fine ivories and sculptures. (Open in season 1000–1800; 2 Nov. to Easter, 1400–1700. Closed Mon. and holidays.) Notable city churches include **St Loup** designed by Pieter Huyssens and **Notre-Dame**.

Namur's Butcher's Hall, built in the Renaissance style of the Meuse region, is today the **Archaeological Museum** with a first-rate collection of Roman, Frankish and Merovingian antiquities from the 1st–7th centuries. **Museum of the Hotel de Croix** is a well-preserved 18th-century building exhibiting 17th- and 18th-century Namur works of art while the **Museum of Classic and Namur Arts** is in another 18th-century patrician house, showing sculptures, paintings and copper objects from the medieval ages and Renaissance periods. (Open 1000–1200; 1400–1600; closed Tues.) Items made by goldsmith, Brother Hugo of Oignies (12th century) can be seen in the Convent of the Sisters of Notre-Dame. (Open 1000–1200; 1400–1600; closed Sun. mornings.)

Namur is a very good base for exploring the Ardennes and is also a popular holiday resort in itself. It has a Théâtre Royal and an open-air theatre, a casino open all year round featuring baccarat and roulette and there are many fine shops on the Rue de L'Ange. *Liège 61km/38mi, Brussels 64km/40mi.*

Philippeville   I5

(pop. 2000) A town founded by order of the Emperor Charles V in 1555 on a high plateau in corn country, designed as the key point for a new defensive system against the French. The old fortifications no longer exist, but the town still possesses several old houses such as the **Maison du Peuple** on the market square – the building where Napoleon spent the night of 19 June when fleeing from Waterloo. *Namur 46km/28mi, Brussels 86km/54mi.*

Rochefort   J11

(pop. 5000) A pretty Ardennes resort and good base for exploring the **Valley of the Lesse**. It is best known for its wild and primitive caves which have particularly deep chambers and galleries like 'The Sabbath Hall'. Cave tours take approximately 75 minutes. The town is an old one and possesses a rustic atmosphere even if many of its buildings, like the town hall and parish church, are in fact, modern. The 13th-century ruined castle has been restored. Men only are allowed inside the Trappist **Abbey of St Remy** (together with

its park, open year round). The Renaissance Chapel of Notre-Dame de Lorette was modelled on Loretto House in Italy. *Dinant 32km/20mi, Brussels 112km/70mi.*

Saint-Hubert   K12

(pop. 3000) A hunting centre in the heart of the Ardennes forest which is the shrine of St Hubert, patron saint of huntsmen and has developed around the Basilica and old Benedictine Abbey. In the fifth chapel in the courtyard on the right hand side of the Basilica (a good example of flamboyant Gothic) are 24 enamel plaques based on engravings by Dürer. The old tomb of the saint is empty and is just a memorial given by Leopold I, himself a great hunter. The saint's relics were buried in the forest during the French invasions, for safe keeping, and were never found afterwards. The 18th-century Abbey buildings are now the province's cultural centre where concerts and exhibitions are regularly given. The flower painter, Redouté, was born in Saint-Hubert and a statue of him stands outside the Town Hall. *Brussels 139km/87mi.*

Spa   F15

(pop 9500) The town destined to add a new word to the dictionaries. Its mineral springs were known in the Middle Ages, but Spa did not acquire a real reputation until the 18th century when the celebrities arrived in droves. Joseph II called it the 'Café of Europe'. Peter the Great was a devotee of Spa as were the first Belgian sovereigns. The properties of the waters are helpful in the treatment of heart complaints and circulation disorders.

Both those seeking cures and tourists who simply enjoy recreational facilities come here. Walk along the promenades: Promenade Meyerbeer, Promenade des Anglais and Promenade des Sept-Heures. Visit the **Museum** which shows a selection of inlaid, hand-painted wooden boxes – for which Spa was famous – dating from the 16th century. Have a flutter in the casino, centrally located, or play golf at the Balmoral Club. Boating is available on the Warfaaz Lake in summer in addition to plentiful terraced cafés, summer theatre, festivals, concerts, exhibitions and sporting events. *Liège 38km/24mi, Brussels 138km/87mi.*

Stavelot   G16

A tourist centre on the edge of the Hautes-Fagnes. It was once best known for its schools and is now known for its tanneries, many of which are delightful old timber-framed houses.

The town's Abbey was founded in 650 by St Remacle, the patron saint; some of its remains can be seen by the banks of the Ambleve as well as the towering porch of the 11th-century romanesque church. Parts of the Abbey buildings, reconstructed in 1783, serve as the Town Hall and the **History Museum**. The Abbey's reliquaries are now kept in the **Church of St Sebastian** (1751), of which the 13th-century reliquary of St Remacle is of particular importance. Made of enamelled and jewelled copper with 12 silver figures of the apostles, it measures 2m/7ft long. Another reliquary, that of St Poppon who built the Abbey Church, is in the form of a bust of that monk, by Jean Gossin in 1626.

Every year Stavelot organizes a famous music festival and at mid Lent, the Blanc Moussis give a joyous carnival atmosphere. Then there are several signposted walks, especially along the Ambleve River. The poet, Guillaume Apollinaire, who spent a summer at a local inn and disappeared without paying his bill, has a museum dedicated to him. (He died in 1918 of war wounds.) *Liège 57km/35mi, Brussels 155km/97mi.*

Verviers   D15

(pop. 56,000) An international textile centre on the Vesdre River. Its Town Hall, Church of Our Lady and several attractive fountains all date from the 18th century.

The theatre here is decorated with murals by Bermans. In the **Municipal Museum** in the Rue Renier, there is a large collection of pictures including those by Patenier and Pourbus. Among modern artists represented are Henri de Braekeleer. *Liège 28km/17.5mi, Brussels 125km/78mi.*

Visé   B14

(pop. 7000) A pretty town on the Meuse. The Town Hall's bulbous belfry tower has a carillon while the **Collegiate Church of St Martin** is a late Gothic building housing the medieval shrine of St Hadelin. The guilds of Visé have preserved ancestral practices, like using cross-bows, which are part of annual fêtes. Water activities such as bathing and canoeing are done from Robinson Beach. *Liège 16km/10mi, Brussels 110km/70mi.*

Yvoir   H8

(pop. 3000) A picturesque Namur town at a river junction with its own castle ruins, waterfall and water mills. Its biggest attraction is the island in the river which has a beach and caters to sports enthusiasts. This is a good base for discovering the **Valley of the Molignée**. Among the features of interest in the general area is the chateau of **Annevoie** which has a lovely water garden designed by Charles-Alexis de Montpellier who closely followed Le Nôtre's work at Versailles. *Dinant 8km/5mi, Brussels 92km/57.5mi.*

The Blancs Moussis, Stavelot

Near Vianden

Echternacht

Clervaux Castle

Clervaux Abbey

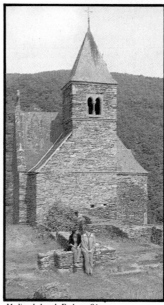

Medieval chapel, Esch-sur-Sûre

LUXEMBOURG

It has been called 'the green heart of Europe' in an age when the phrase referred to its beautiful countryside and not the colour of the money that banking and finance have brought to it, nor the renown achieved through its European Centre, set just outside Luxembourg City on the Kirchberg Plateau.

It is true that Luxembourg has been a prosperous country since the proclamation of its independence in 1867, and the discovery by Gilchrist Thomas, an English engineer, in 1867, of a 'magical formula' for dephosphorizing cast iron which led to a steel industry which has survived the 1970s' crisis better than most.

One thousand years of history have given such a colourful and eventful past to this small state that it benefited more than suffered from successive cultures. Each one left its mark and its relics as a reward for today's tourists to find. Combined, they have produced a strong national unity, an authentic conglomeration of multi-national traits that spells Luxembourg.

If the new industries attract the businessmen, it is romantic and ancient legend which gives this Grand Duchy its international tourist appeal. After all, there are real princes and princesses in this tiny, fairytale, 2586sq.km/999sq.mi. European pocket, guarded by over thirty castles. They perch above green valleys, like Bourscheid; they cling to cliffs like Esch-sur-Sûre above the River Sûre. Not all of them are dark and sombre ruins like Brandenburg, set in its circle of mountains. Luxembourg's finest, Vianden, has been completely restored, and is one of the celebrated visits on any Luxembourg itinerary. Indeed, it was a big attraction even in its ruined state. It is perhaps amusing to note that this particular castle was not naturally ruined! In 1820, in times of economic hardship, one of the city administrators bought the chateau for himself and within seven years had sold the entire copper roof, all the wooden beams and even solid chunks of wall as recycled building material. It was such a scandal that the tourist office likes to keep quiet about it nowadays.

If Vianden is a delightful, historic little town, so is Echternach. The area around it – a hilly, wooded region, criss-crossed by

streams – is known as 'Little Switzerland'. Along with Echternach, Müllerthal, Con-

In Little Switzerland

sdorf and Larochette are all popular summer holiday centres. Their surrounding glens and grottoes provide cool retreat in July and August, the hottest months.

Much of Luxembourg continues to be rustic, both in the rugged mountainous north, an extension of the Belgian Ardennes, and in the more pastoral south. In the centre of the country, there are beautiful valleys like that of the Alzette where Mersch is built. The Alzette is associated with Melusina, the lovely but elusive mermaid who, according to legend, was the wife of Siegfried, Count of the Ardennes and founder of Luxembourg in 963.

Even today, the most evident inhabitants of the northern valleys are deer and wild boar, but wherever you go, you may be sure of river scenery. The hilly E'sleck country, location of Esch-sur-Sûre, is trenched by the Sûre and Our rivers. Their steep slopes are carpeted with spruce and oak and their meadows are scattered with wild flowers. The Lake of the Upper Sûre is a popular recreational area in this region. Luxembourg's main river, however, is the Moselle on whose slopes grow the grapes for the Grand Duchy's famous light, white wines.

Only the capital, Luxembourg City, has any really modern additions and even this city can't lose its medieval past so clearly visible in its churches and other historic buildings. At one time, this capital was one of Europe's most powerful fortresses. The Grand Duchy's visible history stems back far earlier than the Middle Ages. Relics of Roman times and even the Celtic era before that, can be found scattered throughout the country and are particularly noticeable at Mersch and Diekirch.

Folklore is important to the Luxembourger, who is neither terribly Germanic although his country is bounded by Germany to the east, nor French, though the French frontier lies to the south. In fact, the Luxembourger is quite a unique personality, stubborn and interesting.

Wine and fish With good reason, Luxembourgers are proud of their Moselle wines, although they are less known than those of Germany and tend to be less sweet. The region has been producing wine since the 3rd century when the Romans introduced viticulture along the Moselle.

The wines produced today are all dry, white and fruity, but fresh, due to the acids and the organic salts of the grapes. The soil and grape variety gives them a most characteristic bouquet. You can make a wine tasting excursion along a 42km/26mi stretch of vineyards but Grevenmacher and Remich have the largest wine cellars. Visitors are welcomed at both for a tour and sampling and both cities hold wine fairs and festivals during spring and autumn.

The most widely sold Luxembourg wines are: the *Elbling*, a simple dry white and *Rivaner* (made from a cross between the *Riesling* and *Silvaner* grapes) which has its own very pronounced bouquet. Other wines to look for are the Auxerrois, fruity – ideal as an aperitif; *Pinot Blanc*, a refreshing accompaniment to a fish course; *Pinot Gris*, an aromatic wine – ideal for meat dishes; *Riesling* and *Traminer*, good with dessert. Wines are strictly controlled and given a quality grading – *Grand Premier Cru* being the highest.

The country has so many rivers, it is not surprising that fish turns up on many a menu. Between 1 April and 30 September is the season for trout and crayfish. Pike comes from the Sûre, Moselle and Our, along with small fish which are generally served fried. Although fish is a favourite entrée, during the shooting season, civet of hare is a popular dish, and in September, expect to find *quetschentârt* (a slice of plum tart) on the dessert list. Just before Shrovetide, shops sell a special pastry known as *les*

pensées brouillees.

Festivals and Events Easter Monday: the *E'maischen* at Luxembourg City's fish market (the oldest and most romantic part of town but where no fish has been sold for at least a hundred years). It is a bustling market featuring sausage grilling, folk dancing and an almost melodious two-tone cacophany as the children blow into their *pëckvillchen* – a colourful little earthenware bird hand-made by local craftsmen just for this one day. The Grand Ducal family (whose palace is in the heart of this festive area) rarely fail to make an appearance and mix with the crowd. Whit Tuesday: the *Dancing Procession* at Echternach. May 1: grand wine tasting days in the co-operative cellars at Remerschen. First Thursday after Whitsun: wine fair at Wormeldange. A grand wine festival takes place in September at Schwebsingen. (There are many small wine fairs and festivals in the Moselle region in spring and autumn.) Luxembourg's National Day, 23 June, includes a torch-light parade, fireworks and dancing in the streets, in the capital. A late August amusement fair runs for two weeks in Luxembourg City. Summer music festivals are notable in Luxembourg City, Echternach and Wiltz.

Beaufort   110

(pop. 800) A popular summer centre set on a plateau on the edge of the Hallerbach valley in the region known as 'Little Switzerland'. It will be appreciated by anyone who enjoys the outdoors – walking and climbing in particular – since there is a variety of well-kept footpaths leading to magnificent viewing points.

There are two lakeside castles here. One, with an Arcadian Court, dates from the 17th century, but the other, a medieval ruin, is the more imposing. At the latter, you can sample *Cassis du Chateau*, a special liqueur made in Beaufort. *Framboise des Bois*, too, is a local village speciality made from strawberries.

'Little Switzerland' as a whole is a good recreational area, which can offer camping, youth hostel, chalet and hotel accommodation plus a full range of sports facilities. Beaufort and nearby **Berdorf** (two miles away) are both picturesque holiday spots for fresh air enthusiasts as the surrounding countryside encompasses 1214ha/3000 acres of dense pine forests. At Berdorf which overlooks the valleys of the Black Ernz, the Sûre and the Aesbach, there are many well-maintained footpaths through chasms and climbing up to rocky summits for splendid scenic views. The village's

main point of interest is its church whose
Roman altar is sculpted with the figures of
Apollo, Hercules, Minerva and Juno.
Luxembourg City 33km/20mi.

Bourscheid   G7

(pop. 930) One of the charming Ardennes
villages situated on a high plateau above the
River Sûre where there are river beaches.
Dominant feature is Bourscheid Castle,
which looks down at this and neighbouring
villages from its lofty, rocky peak. During
the 12th century, the Lords of Bourscheid
played prominent roles in Luxembourg's,
and indeed, Europe's history, fighting at
both Crécy and Agincourt. Bourscheid is a
popular base for walkers as other villages,
such as **Michelau** and **Goebelsmühle** in
the Sûre valley, and **Welscheid** in the Wark
valley in the area may easily be visited.

Bettembourg   Q8

(pop. 6600) Thousands of families come
here annually to visit the **Park Merveilleux**
– a recreation park that includes a children's playground, game enclosure and
fairytale settings. A mini-train, mini-boats
and mini-golf keep everyone occupied and
concerts are also held here.
Luxembourg City 10km/6mi.

Clervaux   D6

(pop. 1500) One of Luxembourg's best-
known tourist centres with a health-giving
high altitude. Located in a deep narrow
valley of the Little Clerf River in the Ardennes, it is a good base for walking or driving
through the surrounding hills. Clervaux is
an administrative, commercial and education centre, with a good choice of hotels, a
youth hostel and camping site.
   The **castle** here was originally built in the
12th century by Gérard de Clervaux for
defence purposes. Since then it has been
destroyed and rebuilt several times, including the most recent damage in the 1944
Ardennes Offensive. Thanks to clever restoration, today it is one of Luxembourg's
most picturesque. The best view is from the
approaching road before it dips into the
village when the chateau appears as a hud-
dle of charcoal-grey, fairytale roof tops. It
was in this very castle in 1950 that Mrs
Eleanor Roosevelt traced back the 'blue
blood' in the ancestry of her late husband,
Franklin Delano Roosevelt, who was
descended from the aristocratic De Lannoi
family.

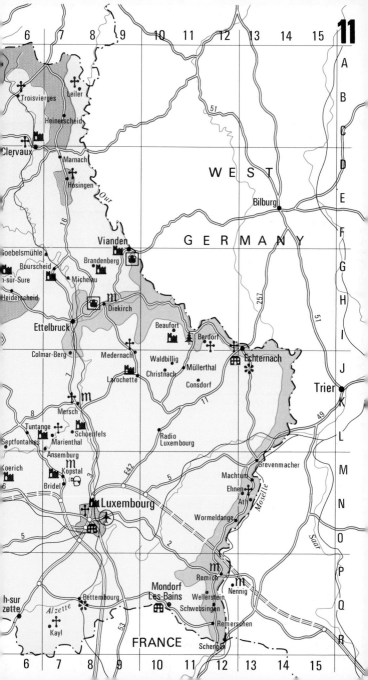

Clervaux

The **Benedictine Abbey** of Sts Maurice and Maur commands the whole valley. Although it was only built in 1910, it was designed in romanesque-Burgundian style by a Dutchman named Klomp. During the last war, it was converted into an Adolf Hitler school. Exhibitions are frequently held in both the abbey and the castle which, along with Clervaux's other major buildings, are floodlit at night in summer. There is an interesting parish church also built in 1910 in a mixture of architectural styles including towers which look quite Rhenish. Also of note in the neighbourhood is the church at **Hachiville** whose architecture, furnishings and frescoes are worth seeing; in particular, the splendidly executed 16th-century Gothic carved wooden altarpiece. It was stolen from the church in 1976 and had to undergo a great deal of restoration when it was found in pieces many months later not far from Clervaux railway station. The **Notre Dame of Lorette** chapel also contains some fine wood carvings. Formerly a place of pilgrimage, this chapel is situated in an attractive park laid out by the De Lannoi family. During the period of French rule it was rumoured that Napoleon attempted to take some of the local deer from the park to his own seat at Fontainebleau. *Luxembourg City 62km/39mi.*

Colmar-Berg   J7

(pop. 1000) The Grand Ducal summer residence in the green and pleasant wooded valley of the Alzette. The nearby Goodyear Tyre Plant and Luxembourg Industries (linen) plant can be visited free upon request by interested groups of people over the age of 17. The maximum number of visitors is fifteen.

Diekirch   H8

(pop. 5600) A key tourist centre on the River Sûre at the foot of the steep Herrenberg – the stronghold of Luxembourg's 600-man army – flanked by orchards and meadows. Luxembourg's tourism began here as it is the meeting point of the Ardennes and the *Bon Pays* to the south, so all kinds of beauty spots abound in the vicinity.

There are well-marked walks from Diekirch – 90km/56mi of them – including a planned nature trail and from town a cycling track stretches to Echternach and Vianden.

All kinds of sports are catered for here, including rod fishing – open to everyone for the price of an ordinary permit. You can play chess outdoors on a giant paving stone chessboard, watch a game of *pétanque* (bowls), go boating or horse riding, play tennis or mini-golf.

Accommodation is plentiful in hotels or camp sites.

Diekirch's famous brewery is certainly worth a visit. Ask for a Diekirch Grand Réserve beer – that's the best. Fish from the

Echternach

region's rivers abound on restaurant menus. Principal historic sites are: the Roman mosaics in the **Municipal Museum**; the **Devil's Altar**, a two thousand year old Celtic monument; and an interesting 9th-century church.
Luxembourg City 35km/21mi.

Echternach   I13

(pop. 4200) A picturesque medieval town on the bank of the Sûre which forms the frontier with Germany. Rich in culture and folklore, atmospheric Echternach has something for everyone. Wander around the narrow streets and ancient ramparts and take a look at the surviving patrician houses. The town is dominated by an old Benedictine abbey founded in the 7th century by Anglo-Saxon St Willibrord, although its four wings built round a large square courtyard were erected at a much later date. At one time the monastery was a powerful European scholastic centre, but when the monks were driven out in 1794 its fame went with them. The **Basilica**, Luxembourg's most important religious building, was almost completely destroyed in 1944 but has since been restored. Its crypt is the original, however, housing the magnificent white marble sarcophagus containing the remains of St Willibrord, and its vaults are painted with frescoes dating back to 1100. Unfortunately, little remains of the once sumptuous 18th-century monastic gardens – just an orangery with alcoved figures and a little rococo pavilion.

The old parish **Church of St Peter and St Paul**, largely designed in romanesque style, stands on a slight hill in the middle of town and is reputed to be the country's oldest Christian sanctuary. The remarkable little **Town Hall** on the Place du Marché (market place) dates from the 15th century and has an arcade and Gothic turrets. There is a lovely Louis XV pavilion in the park.

A popular excursion area from town is the **Müllerthal**, a deep, rocky valley, known as Luxembourg's 'Little Switzerland'. Quiet scenic beauty can be found in Echternach's wooded surrounds which are criss-crossed by streams and studded with waterfalls. The artificial lake in Echternach is used in summer for swimming and boating and if it freezes in winter it provides a unique open-air ice skating rink. There's a good choice of accommodation and entertainments especially in summer when a number of concerts is held here. Over the last few years, Echternach has become quite celebrated as a music centre.

Traditions remain strong here, especially amongst old stock Echternachers who still tend to shun modern medical practitioners. They say they'd rather trust the concoctions which have been mixed and brewed for years by one of the old Echternach publicans whose pub has therefore become known as *the doctor's*! Whit Tuesday: **Dancing Procession**, pilgrimage to the tomb of St Willibrord.
Luxembourg City 34km/21mi.

Esch-sur-Sûre   G5

(pop. 250) A medieval village with a fairy-tale appearance in one of the country's most impressive settings. It is built on a small peninsula in the loop of the River Sûre surrounded by steep crags giving the impression it is an island. A cluster of houses cling to a rock once crowned by a mighty castle (now ruined) while forbidding cliffs drop almost vertically to the river below. It was from this castle that Henri d'Esch left to accompany Godfrey de Bouillon on the First Crusade. In summer it is floodlit.

Esch-sur-Sûre

There are some unusual chapels in the vicinity, notably the octagonal chapel of **Heiderscheidergrund**; 30km/19mi of footpaths with viewing points along the way; and plenty of sport possibilities. Weekly concerts start here in June and accommodation is available in holiday cottages, private houses, hotels and camp sites. Esch-sur-

Sûre is reached by passing through a tunnel constructed in 1850.
Luxembourg City 45km/28mi.

Grevenmacher   M13

(pop. 3000) Capital of the Moselle wine growing region on the eastern border of Luxembourg. Take the *wine road* and make

Esch-sur-Sûre

a definite stop here to tour its wine cellars. The first co-operative winery was set up in Grevenmacher in 1921. In addition to the co-operative wine cellars, you can also visit those of Bernard-Massard, whose sparkling wines (Luxembourg's equivalent of champagne) have been popular with wine drinkers for over fifty years.

The town itself boasts few medieval remains, only some old walls which form part of cottages and a long crude staircase which leads up to the chapel and calvary at the top of Kreuzerberg Hill. Wine Fair on the Thursday after Easter. *Luxembourg City 28km/17.5mi.*

Heinerscheid   C7

(pop. 950) A well-known highland village which together with nearby **Leiler**, stands above the romantic valleys of the Upper Our and the Clerf. If you enjoy fresh air and rural surroundings, both these villages are good starting points for walkers, and you will find many ideal picnic spots. Leiler's 14th-century Gothic church is worth a

visit as it contains some interesting ancient frescoes.

Hosingen   E7

(pop. 550) A village, situated in the beautiful valley of the Our, which was largely destroyed during the 1944 Ardennes Offensive but has since been rebuilt. The only surviving originals in the convent church (12th-century foundations) on a large central market square are the baroque altars. Most of the fittings, including the mosaic Stations of the Cross, are new.

Insenborn-Lultzhausen   H4

(pop. 145) This is a good base for young people who enjoy an active holiday. This area is near the Upper Sûre Lake and features wide panoramas and marvellous views. There are plenty of well-marked walks in the region and the lake itself is a good place for water sports such as boating, swimming and sub-aqua.

River Sûre

Kayl   R7

(pop. 6500) A small town located at the
entry of the valley of the Kayl and surrounded by thick woods and rugged hills.
The town of Kayl is best known for its
Sanctuary of Our Lady of the Miners with
its national monument erected in honour of
1400 miners who died here.
Luxembourg City 21km/13mi.

Koerich   M5

Situated on the fringe of the Eisch valley,
Koerich has its own ruined castle and an
adjacent baroque church with onion-
shaped spire and handsome 18th-century
carved wooden altar. The Maison Henn-
Eischen and its furniture were designed by
the same craftsmen.

Kopstal   M7

(pop. 2500) In the heart of the Mamer
valley, Kopstal and sister town, **Bridel**, are
both bases for exploring a network of tourist routes in the valley. Situated on a sunny
plateau, they are within easy access of prehistoric caves, Celtic huts, Roman temple
remains and a good smattering of ruined
feudal castles.

Larochette   J9

(pop. 1400) A quaint old market town in
scenic 'Little Switzerland', nestled in a narrow wooded valley where the White Ernz
stream descends from the Grunewald. The
valley is overlooked by two ruined medieval
castles, linked by a curtain wall, which were
destroyed by fire in 1565. In the town's
main square there's an old Cross of Justice –
a feature of Luxembourg towns. Judicial
pronouncements used to be made here.

Larochette is probably preferable slightly out of season as, in summer, tourists,
particularly from Belgium and Holland,
love to walk through its surrounding woods
and glens. Facilities include mini-golf,
campsite, hotel and apartment accommodation.

One of the recommended walking tours
from Larochette is that of the Manzelbach.
This long path through the woods leads to a
Cinderella-type castle called **Meysembourg**, an imposing structure built at the
turn of the century on the site of the old
Meysembourg château dating back to 1176.
Forest entirely surrounds the castle which
is inhabited by the Princesse d'Arenberg
and is not open to the public. Another

recommended excursion takes you to the
village of **Medernach** whose church has a
rococo altarpiece and furniture designed in
the 18th century by the Bavarian,
Paulys Courtz, a Franciscan novice of
Diekirch. *Luxembourg City 25km/15mi.*

Luxembourg City   O8

(pop. 78,000) For a thousand years this has
been the capital of the Grand Duchy of
Luxembourg and is still the home of the
Grand Duke and his family. For centuries it
was one of the world's most powerful fortresses and, indeed, only some one hundred
years ago actually gave up its heritage as a
fortress city and opened up its bastions. (It
was dismantled between 1867 and 1883.)

Luxembourg's success in the financial
sector lies in its holding company laws, its
very liberal foreign exchange system and its
easy-going stock exchange regulations. At
present, there are over 3000 holding companies established in the capital which has
developed into a major financial centre
thanks mainly to the strong expansion of its
banking structure over the past three de-
cades.

For the tourist, however, it is the city's
tumultuous and historic past which is the
most interesting. It is still quite evident in
the old quarter since many relics have been
preserved including the **Citadel of St
Esprit** itself and the remains of the Castle
on the Bock. Although these massive fortifications have nowadays become parks, the
Bock is still shrouded in legend. For example, Siegfried's wife, Melusina, the lovely
mermaid, supposedly appears every 1000
years bearing a key to unknown treasures.
The last time she was supposed to make this
appearance was in 1963 when the local
parish priest of the ancient church of St
Michael locked the door lest anyone should
see her – or perhaps to keep the legend
going! In either case, you'll have a long time
to wait before she's next due to show her-
self.

What to See Most of the striking old parts
of the city are in the lower town in the valley
of the Alzette. From here, there are plenty
of fine vistas across the ravine which is
bridged by a great single-arched bridge, the
Pont Adolphe, 46m/150ft high and 84m/
275ft wide, plus a sturdy multi-arched
viaduct called the Passerelle, built when
Luxembourg was still a fortress. In actual
fact, Luxembourg City is a city of bridges –
there are some 101 including the new
Grande Duchess Charlotte Bridge, known
as the Red Bridge because of its colour —
not any political overtones — spanning the
355m/1165ft of one of the valleys over

Luxembourg at dawn

which the city extends. This bridge is 85m/
278ft high and there are another four massive viaducts up to 43m/140ft high.

Visit the **Casemates**, a 21km/13mi network of subterranean passages hewn from
solid rock and walk along the unique **Promenade de la Corniche**, a fine scenic road
which almost encircles the town. Viewed
from the Corniche, it is easy to note the
contrast between the old and new sections
of town. For instance, the banking quarter,
Luxembourg's Wall Street, shows the latest
in office architecture once you reach Boulevard Royal. The new bank towers are higher than Notre Dame's spires, even though
that cathedral is but a stone's throw away.
The nucleus of the old town is indeed the
Cathedral of Notre Dame (1613–1621)
which has good sculptures and a crypt containing the Grand Ducal mausoleum and
the tomb of John the Blind, King of Bohemia and Count of Luxembourg, who died
heroically fighting against the English at
the Battle of Crécy, and from whom the
Black Prince is said to have adopted his
emblem: three feathers and the phrase 'Ich
dien – I serve', which is still the emblem
and motto of Britain's Prince Charles.

Next door to the cathedral is the former
Jesuit College, now the National Library.
Nearby is the **Grand Ducal Palace**, open to
visitors for guided tours in summer. Part
was built in the 16th century and part in the
19th. The older portion is remarkable in its
Renaissance style. Built at the time of the
Spanish occupation, it has the same strange
Moorish carvings as found in the cathedral.
At one time, the palace was the town hall.
Today's town hall (1830–8) overlooks Place
Guillaume with its equestrian statue of Wil-
liam II. In the vicinity are several elegant
ministries, many of them 18th-century.
Here, too, is St Michael's Church and
another tiny ancient chapel, St Quirin's
(14th-century) built into the rock in the
valley.

Other points of special interest are the
two old town gateways, the towers of the
Rham, the Three Acorns and elegant
Spanish turrets. From the Bock Plateau, a
monument acts as reminder that Goethe
stayed twice in Luxembourg in 1792. From
the same plateau, many of the suburbs are
visible. In one of them, **Hamm**, just outside
the city, General Patton is buried in the
American military cemetery. (He did not

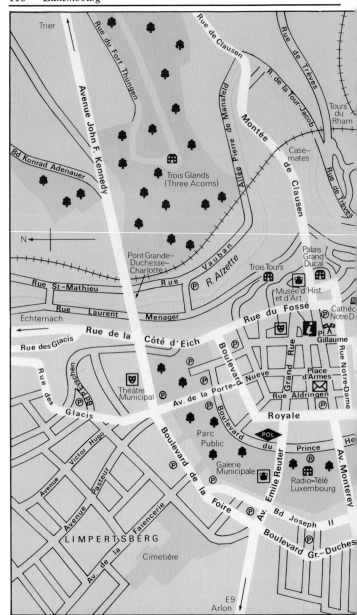

Trier

Rue du Fort Thüngen

Rue de Clausen

Rue de Trèves

Avenue John F. Kennedy

Bd Konrad Adenauer

Tours du Rham

Trois Glands
(Three Acorns)

R. de la Tour-Jacob

Allée Pierre de Mansfeld

Montée de Clausen

Case-mates

Rue de Trèves

N

Pont Grande-Duchesse-Charlotte

Vauban

R. Alzette

Trois Tours

Palais Grand Ducal

Rue St-Mathieu

Rue

Musée d'Hist. et d'Art

Cathéd Notre D

Rue   Laurent   Menager

Echternach

Rue du Fossé

Rue de la   Côté d'Eich

Pl. Gillaume

Rue des Glacis

Boulevard

Grand   Rue

Rue Notre-Dame

Rue des

Théâtre Municipal

Av. de la Porte   Nueve

Place d'Armes

Rue Aldringen

Glacis

Royale

Bd. Eechen

Boulevard

POL

Prince

He

Avenue Victor Hugo

Parc Public

du

Émile Reuter

Av. Monterey

Avenue Pasteur

Galerie Municipale

Radio-Télé Luxembourg

Boulevard de la   Foire

Av. de la   Faïencerie

LIMPERTSBERG

Cimetière

Av. Bd Joseph II

Boulevard Gr.-Duches

E9
Arlon

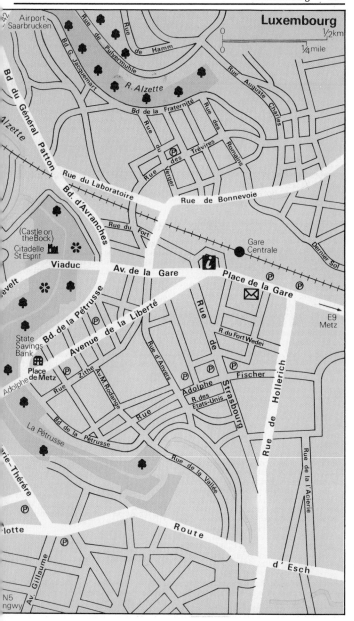

Luxembourg

Airport Saarbrücken

Rue de Hamm

Bd G. Jacquemart

R. Alzette

Rue Auguste Charles

Bd du Général Patton

Bd de la Fraternité

Rue des

Rue du Laboratoire

Bd d'Avranches

Rue du Fort

Rue de Bonnevoie

Rue des Trévires

Rue des Romains

Rue Werner

Rue du Fort

(Castle on the Bock)
Citadelle St Esprit

Viaduc

Gare Centrale

Derner Sol

Av. de la Gare

Place de la Gare

Bd de la Pétrusse

Av. de la Liberté

Avenue de la Liberté

Rue

de

E9 Metz

State Savings Bank

Place de Metz

Zithe

Av M Rodange

Rue d'Anvers

R. du Fort Wedel

Rue

Adolphe

R. des Etats-Unis

Fischer

Strasbourg

Rue de Hollerich

Rue de la Pétrusse

Bd de la Pétrusse

La Pétrusse

Rue de la Vallée

Route

d' Esch

Rue de la l'Acierie

rie-Thérère

lotte

N5 ngwy

Av Gillaume

Adolphe

Roosevelt

Alzette

die in the last war, but in a car crash in the environs of Luxembourg.) In another cemetery, that of Limpertsberg, another popular 'military' hero lies buried: Wilhelm Voigt, the cobbler who featured in European history as *Der Hauptmann von Küpenick* and became the model for Karl-Zuckmeyer's film-operetta of the same name. Posing as a military commander, he had conned the Prussian army into officially handing over the *Reichskasse*, a state reserve fund, to him for safe custody.

New Luxembourg City is mainly on the upper level. Place d'Armes (near the palace) is a social hub. Sit at one of the tree-shaded cafés and watch whatever's going on, which might include open-air summer concerts. Many of the principal new buildings, including the headquarters of Radio Luxembourg, are situated in or near the park here, along with the Municipal Theatre flanked by its monument honouring Robert Schuman, one of the founders of the European Community. Located in the Place de Metz and overlooking the main valley, in the centre of the city stands the imposing National Savings Bank which many tourists instinctively mistake for the Grand Ducal Palace. The old fish market (Marché aux poissons) is today just another square, site of the once-a-year **E'Maischen market** when unique pottery is for sale, made by the people of old Luxembourg and Nospelt. The **State Museum** is here, with fine collections of art, archaeology and natural history.

Where to stay There are only two luxury hotels in Luxembourg City. However, there are several modern establishments with good facilities in the de luxe category. Among those recommended: the Hotel Aerogolf Sheraton, close to the airport; the Cravat which probably has the best location overlooking the valley, and often used by diplomats; the Holiday Inn, close to the EEC Centre; and the Nobilis, the city's newest, near the station. On a secondary level, the Kons, opposite the station, and the Rix in the centre of town, are both good. The average tourist might choose the Dauphin, the International, the Schintgen or the Carlton. Two others worth mentioning are the San Remo on Place Guillaume and the Hôtel du Théâtre.

Eating out You will find Germanic and French influences in Luxembourg City's restaurants. Coq-au-vin is a speciality of the exclusive Gourmet in Rue Chimay. Other expensive restaurants include the Astoria, the Cordial, the St Michel, Des Empereurs and the Um Bock. Among the less pricey are: Don Quixote, La Marmite, La Poele d'Or, the President, which has turn-of-the-century train décor, and the Mansfeld which serves local specialities and has a

most lively atmosphere.

Entertainment Most Luxembourgers prefer socializing in a café to anything else when it comes to spending an evening out. Nightlife *per se*, therefore, is a bit on the staid side although there are some nightclubs. For cabaret, try the Splendide or the Golden Club (which has gold-plated taps in the toilets). Others which are reasonable are the Plaza and the Bugatti. The Scorpio is a disco. Trendiest addition to the pub scene with regular live entertainment is The Cockpit, decorated with bits and pieces of aeroplanes.

Most of the city residents are very sport oriented which accounts for the large number of sports clubs. Visitors can join most of them reasonably easily, saving the Grand Ducal Golf Club.
Brussels 219km/137mi.

Marienthal   J7

Situated in the peaceful valley of the Eisch at the foot of the undamaged mighty Hollenfels Castle (which now houses a very active youth hostel) and quite close to the elegant estate and Château of Ansembourg. It is renowned for its little old monastery of the **Pères Blancs** which used to be a school for missionaries to Africa and which now houses a small colonial museum. The sanctuary and its gardens are just right for the traveller who wants a few minutes of total relaxation to meditate – and wonder why perhaps Luxembourg's oldest registered liqueur is in fact called *Grand Liqueur du Père Blanc*!

Mersch   K7

(pop. 4000) A bright little town at the crossroads of several tourist routes in the centre of the Grand Duchy and at the entrance to what is known as the Valley of the Seven Castles (the Eisch). It has a couple of churches worth seeing and its own château (although the latter pales in comparison to those in the valley). Mersch is the starting-point for a visit to the **Hunnebour's Springs**, the prehistoric caves at **Mamer** and the Roman villa at **Dreibouren**.
Luxembourg City 17km/10mi.

Mondorf-les-Bains   Q10

(pop. 2000) A pleasant spa situated in the valley of the Gander which forms the frontier with French Lorraine. The thermal establishment and new centre is fed by two springs and deals with liver, gall bladder, stomach and intestinal complaints plus rheumatism in all its forms. With or without the mineral waters, this is an attractive place to stay. There is a casino in park surroundings and guided walks are available as is bike rental. *Son et lumière* presentations are given in the parish church on Friday evenings.

What most tourists do not know is that Luxembourg's strongest man (indeed, one of the world's) was born, brought up and lies buried in Mondorf. His name was John Gruen (1868–1912) and he toured Europe and America performing such feats of strength as breaking horseshoes, lifting 25 people standing on a platform, and two horses plus their riders. He held the world record at one time by being capable of lifting 1814kg/4000lb.
Luxembourg City 20km/12.5mi.

The Casino, Mondorf-les-Bains

Remerschen R12

(pop. 600) A well-known wine centre on the banks of the Moselle. There is a small 18th-century chapel in its narrow main street, **Caves Co-operatives de Sud** which hold 55,000 hectolitres/968,000pts and may be visited. Two other wine centres in the immediate vicinity are **Schengen** and **Wintrange**. A bridge links Schengen to the German bank of the Moselle. Grand Wine tasting day May 1.

Remich P12

(pop. 2400) An important wine and commercial centre situated on the European Highway at the foot of vine-covered slopes on the banks of the Moselle. It is the Seat of the State Viticulture Institute and the National Wine Mark. You can visit both co-operative and private cellars. There is sparkling wine at Caves St Martin and a wine tasing pavilion at Caves St Remy.

Remich has Roman origins. It still boasts some old walls and a gateway bridging a narrow street. A wide tree-shaded promenade runs beside the river where pleasure boats ply. There's also an open-air chess game here. Germany is within such easy access it is worth crossing the bridge to see the mosaics in the Roman villa at **Nennig**. Remich is also the starting point for excursions on the Moselle. Wine Festival: 21 July.
Luxembourg City 23km/14mi.

Septfontaines L5

(pop. 500) A spot in the centre of the wooded Eisch valley dominated by its own medieval castle (Septfontaines). From here, you could walk to all seven castles in the Eisch valley, like Schoenfels, for example, which is overlooked by a hill punctuated by many caves where an early race of dwarfs known as *Little People* are said to have lived. Septfontaines, of course, is named for the town's own seven fountains and it also has a Gothic style church worth seeing.

There are many true tales of *wonder-doctoring* about this region. This might have had something to do with the fact that, up until the 1930s when the new pharmaceutical industry sprang up, the large scale cultivation of medicinal plants and herbs had been a major form of livelihood in the area of 'Simmerschmelz'.
Luxembourg City 21km/13mi.

Troisvierges B6

(pop. 1000) A welcoming, friendly tourist centre in the northern Ardennes region, set amid woods, meadows and moors, with its own leisure and sports centre. From July to September, there are organized hiking tours from here. The town has a beautiful **parish church** noted for its remarkably high altar, its outstanding Stations of the Cross, exquisite baroque church furniture and paintings by pupils of Rubens.

See also the **Franciscan Monastery** (1630) and 5km/3mi away, the hermitage chapel of Hachiville. 8km/5mi away is Luxembourg's highest peak, the **Buurgplaatz** which, however, does not provide the same magnificent, unobstructed panorama which the Grand Duchy's second highest point, the **Napoléonsgaard** does, in the Rindschleiden area near **Grevels**. Second Sunday in September: Festival of the Heather.
Luxembourg City 46km/28mi.

Vianden

Vianden   F9

(pop. 1600) 'If I had to see only one castle, one landscape and one town, it is Vianden that I would choose. It is at one and the same time the most elaborate and wildest spot to be seen on this side of the Rhine. The castle is enormous; it is one with the rock, then draws its towers away to rear them toward heaven. At its feet, the village tumbles down the slopes in little medieval streets. Nothing has changed since the times when Victor Hugo, a voluntary exile, came here to meditate and dream in a framework worthy of his genius.'

A modern writer said this and this is one of the Grand Duchy's most famous beauty spots, whose formidable castle has only just been completely restored. The castle was one of the largest feudal fortresses in the Eifel and Ardennes area – perhaps in Western Europe. The Orange-Nassau dynasty was born here through the marriage of Countess Adelaide of Vianden to Count Othon de Nassau-Dillenbourg. She was one of the members of the notable family who lived in the château in the 14th century. The royal family of Holland is directly descended from this line.

Vianden was built in the 9th century on the banks of the Our and its scenery is wildly romantic. Its single street (as the above writer suggests) appears to plunge down the hillside, cobbled and full of character, to cross the river and form a tiny bulge into Germany. Many of the 18th-century houses which lined it, have sur-

vived. Some of their doors are decorated with sculpted clusters of fruit like the one where Luxembourg's poet, Edmond de la Fontaine lived. Others have vaulted entrance halls and passages, like the one which is now the **Folklore Museum** (containing some good antiques and period furniture). The **Victor Hugo Museum** is the former house of the famous French writer who spent part of his exile from France here in Vianden. Both the house (which used to belong to a local grocer in Hugo's time) and the little bridge nearby, guarded by the petrified figure of St Nicholas were war damaged and have since been restored.

While in Vianden, Hugo wrote much of his best poetry and sketched all the local castles, not to mention, installing two of his mistresses in adjoining quarters. It was the poet who said 'Before long the whole of Europe will visit Vianden, this jewel set in its splendid scenery . . . and its cheerful breed of men.'

He has been proved right. There are comfortable hotels here today and, as a sign of our times, a huge hydro-electric pumping works – Europe's most powerful.

Considering that the **Siegfried Line** (practically naked rock now) lies just over the river on the German side, it is hardly surprising that much of Vianden was damaged in World War II. However, the parish church is reasonably good 13th-century Gothic and does contain the original stalls and tomb of Count Henri of Nassau. Outside of Vianden there are other castles

worth visiting, two notable ones being on German soil. Across the river is **Roth**, a fortified religious house of the Knights Templar, and at **Falkenstein** high above the German bank, to the north, is an eagle's nest of a castle, clearly seen from the little chapel of the Bildchen perched high on the Vianden side. Take the chairlift to this excellent viewing point.
Luxembourg City 46km/28mi.

Waldbillig   J10

(pop. 265) One of four villages at the end of the 'wine road' and the start of 'Little Switzerland' – or the *Müllerthal*. It lies in a pocket of ravines, strange rock formations, streams and quiet woods with views over silent valleys and hills. Walks may be taken through the glens. The other villages are: **Müllerthal** itself, **Christnach** and **Haller**.

Wellenstein   Q12

(pop. 440) A village of Luxembourg's Moselle region. Set in the middle of vineyards a little way back from the river, it has some important wine cellars. From the Scheuerberg there is a vast panorama of the Moselle valley. Several other villages in the vicinity are worth seeing: nearby **Bech-Kleinmacher** is one of the oldest wine centres where a 350-year-old brewer's house, called a *possen*, has a wine and folklore museum. **Schwebsingen**, a pretty village on the banks of the Moselle, full of flowers, has an open-air museum exhibiting antique wooden and stone wine presses, plus sculptures in the vineyard. There is a new harbour here for pleasure boating and comfortable hiking trails through the surrounding forest.

Wiltz   F4

(pop. 4000) Capital of the Ardennes region, this town was at the middle of the 1944–45 Battle of the Bulge. Today Wiltz is an international meeting place for scouts, with plenty of camping and chalet accommodation. It is also a key centre for classical music and drama in summer with its festival staged in the open-air theatre of the château.

The town is divided into two by the Wiltz river. The lower town takes up part of the wide valley, while the upper town has its inevitable medieval castle and a church containing tombstones of the feudal Counts of Wiltz. The traditional Cross of Justice (1502), monuments and remnants of the Second World War can be found here, too, including a **Museum of the Battle of the Bulge**.

Wiltz is an ideal centre for sports enthusiasts. Rowing, archery, sailing, swimming and tennis may all be enjoyed here and its high altitude gives it a healthy climate. Wiltz makes its own excellent beer and the fresh trout caught from the river is first class.
Luxembourg City 54km/34mi.

Wormeldange   O12

(pop. 1100) Capital of Riesling, one of four neighbouring wine centres along the Moselle below vine-covered slopes. Visit the co-operative caves which can store as much as 3 million litres/5¼ million pints of wine, and the St Doanat Chapel on the Koeppchen for a panoramic view. Just below Wormeldange, **Ehnen**, a tiny medieval hamlet with an enchanting atmosphere, boasts the Grand Duchy's only secular church dedicated to St Nicholas, the patron saint. The two other wine centres are **Ahn** and **Machtum**.

Wiltz

INDEX

The index is in four separate parts. The first part (below) refers to all the general information in the book. Each of the three countries has its own index which refers to the gazetteer. In all four indexes all the main entries are printed in heavy type. Map references are also printed in heavy type. The map number precedes the grid reference.

BELGIUM

HOLLAND

LUXEMBOURG